TIERED FLUENCY INSTRUCTION

Supporting Diverse Learners in Grades 2–5

BY CHASE YOUNG AND TIMOTHY RASINSKI

MAUPIN HOUSE BY
CAPSTONE PROFESSIONAL
a capstone imprint

Tiered Fluency Instruction: Supporting Diverse Learners in Grades 2–5
By Chase Young and Timothy Rasinski

Cover Design: Charmaine Whitman and Lisa King
Book Design: Lisa King

Library of Congress Cataloging-in-Publication Data
Names: Young, Chase. | Rasinski, Timothy V.
Title: Tiered fluency instruction : supporting diverse learners in grades
2–5 / by Chase Young and Timothy Rasinski.
Description: North Mankato, Minnesota : Capstone Press, 2017. | Includes
    bibliographical references.
Identifiers: LCCN 2016014664| ISBN 9781496608031 (pbk.) | ISBN
9781496608048   (ebook (pdf))
Subjects: LCSH: Reading. | Reading—Remedial teaching.
Classification: LCC LB1050 .Y685 2017 | DDC 372.4—dc23
LC record available at https://lccn.loc.gov/2016014664

Image Credits:
iStockphoto/urbancow, cover, back cover; Timothy Rasinski and Chase Young,
96–99

Capstone Professional publishes professional resources for K–12 educators.
Contact us for tailored, in-school training or to schedule an author for a workshop
or conference. Visit www.capstonepd.com for free lesson plan downloads.

This book includes websites that were operating at the time it went to press.

Maupin House Publishing, Inc. by Capstone Professional
1710 Roe Crest Drive
North Mankato, MN 56003
www.capstonepd.com
888-262-6135
info@capstonepd.com

TABLE OF CONTENTS

INTRODUCTION

Over the past several decades, reading fluency has been neglected and misunderstood, and, as a result, reading fluency instruction in many classrooms has been ignored or implemented in ways that are not necessarily good instruction (Rasinski, 2012). For example, many teachers complain about having to do daily "timed readings" in their classrooms, in which students are prompted to read as quickly as possible, all in the name of developing reading fluency.

We feel that this neglect and misinterpretation of reading fluency is truly regrettable as a growing body of research has acknowledged that 1) reading fluency is essential to students' reading development, and 2) a large number of students who struggle in reading exhibit difficulties in one or more areas of reading fluency. We can't help but wonder that if reading fluency were made to be a truly essential and authentic component of the reading curriculum, students' overall reading proficiency would increase and the number of students experiencing difficulty in reading would decline substantially.

> ... a large number of students who struggle in reading exhibit difficulties in one or more areas of reading fluency.

That is the hope of this book. In writing this book, we hope to provide you with a compendium or toolkit of fluency strategies that you can employ with students in grades two through five to improve their reading fluency, and in turn, increase their overall reading proficiency. Moreover, we have organized, or tiered, the fluency strategies around the individual and group needs of the students you work with. In this way, you are more able to choose fluency instruction that will best meet the needs of your students. More about the tiers is discussed later in this introduction.

What Is Fluency?

Let's begin with a brief explanation of reading fluency. Essentially, we see reading as having two major components—a surface component and a deep component (Rasinski, 2010). The deep component of reading refers to comprehension or meaning. Readers have to use their cognitive resources to dig for and uncover the meaning that an author has embedded in her or his text. The deep reading component is the goal of all reading—to discover meaning in a text.

The surface component refers more to the mechanical tasks of reading—to decode the words in text as accurately and as effortlessly as possible and to read with expression to enhance the meaning of the text. Although we often think of expressive reading as happening only during oral reading, we feel that expressive reading happens during silent reading as well, especially if the reader is proficient in his or her reading. While, in a sense, the surface component of reading is less important than the deep component, it is essential for proficiency in reading. In order for readers to get to the deep level, they need to master the surface component first. Have you ever observed a reader who struggles in word decoding skills or who reads in a monotone, word-by-word manner? Chances are those readers struggle in making meaning as well.

Word recognition is clearly critical for reading. One cannot read if he or she is unable to turn the printed version of words into their oral equivalent, like a story that is heard. Developing proficiency in decoding words accurately is not sufficient, however. Word recognition must be developed to a point of automatic or effortless word decoding. The theory of automaticity suggests that all readers have a limited amount of cognitive resources or cognitive energy to put toward understanding what they read (LaBerge & Samuels, 1974). Essentially, cognitive energy refers to the mental manipulations we go through in solving a problem. That energy can be applied to a variety of tasks. However, because we have a limited amount of this energy, it needs to be used efficiently. Reading is a multitask activity. We think you will agree that proficient reading requires a reader to first decode the words encountered in print (surface task) and to next make sense of what the author is saying with the words (deep task). If a reader has to use too much cognitive energy to decode the words, less cognitive energy is available for comprehension. The students who read words in text correctly but in an overly labored, halting, and sluggish manner are using too much of their cognitive energy to decode the words. As a result, little energy is left for comprehension and it falters.

Our goal for word recognition should be accuracy and automaticity (LaBerge & Samuels, 1974). When something is done automatically, it is done with little cognitive effort. So many things in life are done automatically: walking down the street, driving a car, brushing our teeth. We often do these tasks without paying much attention to doing them. The result is that we can usually multitask: walk down the street and chat with a friend, appreciate the scenery, think about a problem. When word recognition is developed to an accurate and automatic level, the reader can devote his or her attention to the more important, deep-level task of comprehension. The best example of a reader who is automatic is most likely you reading this page. You do not have to analyze or sound out every word on the page. Rather, you are instantly and effortlessly recognizing the words and thus are better able to pay attention to the meaning we are attempting to share with you. Research has demonstrated that accuracy and automaticity in word recognition are strongly correlated with good comprehension. The better readers are at accurate and automatic word recognition, the more proficient they are in reading comprehension.

> *When word recognition is developed to an accurate and automatic level, the reader can devote his or her attention to the more important, deep-level task of comprehension.*

And so, the first major component of fluency is accurate and automatic word recognition. And, like walking or driving a car or brushing our teeth, both accuracy and automaticity are developed through lots of practice.

The second major component of reading fluency is expression in oral reading (Schreiber, 1980). The technical term for reading with good expression is *prosody*. Consider this: The most fluent speaker you can think of is one who speaks with appropriate expression, holds your attention, and enhances the meaning of her or his speech. Now think of a less-than-fluent speaker, one who speaks in a slow, monotone manner. Chances are you have difficulty keeping your attention on the message of the speaker and are less likely to understand what that person may be saying.

The same is true in reading. Readers who read with good expression are reflecting and enhancing the meaning of the text they are encountering. Readers who read with poor expression are less likely to understand the text they are reading. Expression includes reading with appropriate volume and confidence, raising and lowering the pitch of one's voice appropriately, pausing at appropriate places in the text, phrasing the text into meaningful units, emphasizing particular words and phrases, and reading with a rate or speed that enhances meaning—slowing down and speeding up as necessary. As with word recognition, research has demonstrated that expression is correlated with overall reading proficiency. Readers who read with good expression tend to be proficient readers even when reading silently, and those who read with minimal expression tend to be less proficient readers even when reading silently.

So we view word recognition and expression as the two critical components of fluency. Developing these components will allow readers to go deep into meaning and become more proficient readers. In the following chapters, we will share with you lessons for developing fluency competency among your students.

Tiers of Fluency Instruction

One of the unique features of this book is that we have sorted the fluency lessons into three tiers. In doing so, we provide you with a way to differentiate the fluency instruction you wish to provide to your students and meet the needs of individuals and groups of students with whom you work. The Response to Intervention framework (RTI) is a multilevel prevention and intervention system consisting of three tiers. All students begin on the first tier and receive research-based general instruction from the teacher. Generally, we understand this as the regular classroom curriculum or instruction. The second tier is for students who do not respond to Tier 1 instruction. These students may be slightly behind their peers or grade-level expectations, indicating the need for additional support. Tier 2 instruction is typically offered in a small group setting, and the interventions are always research based, which aim to close the gap between their performance and grade-level expectations. Finally, students who still demonstrate difficulty ascend to Tier 3. On this tier, we offer intense, research-based instruction that is proven to rapidly increase reading proficiency. Many times, Tier 3 students receive one-on-one instruction provided by the classroom teacher or reading specialist (National Center on Response to Intervention, 2010).

Tier 1

Tier 1 fluency instruction could be given to all students in a classroom. It is the type of instruction that could easily fit into a regular classroom curriculum and may include many of the types of activities that you already engage in with your students. All students need some degree of fluency instruction, and Tier 1 instruction fits those needs.

Tier 2

Tier 2 fluency instruction is intended for students who may need a bit of a boost in fluency. Students who could benefit from Tier 2 fluency instruction may be developing as readers. However, their fluency development may not be as robust as you would like. Continued lagging in fluency may eventually result in these students requiring more intense intervention in reading, not only in fluency but in other areas as well. Because fluency is, in a sense, a gateway to deeper levels of proficiency in reading, difficulties in fluency may eventually result in other competencies being underdeveloped. The notion behind Tier 2 fluency instruction is to intervene early enough and with sufficient intensity to overcome fluency concerns before they lead to other more significant reading problems.

Tier 3

Some students unfortunately do not develop well in fluency, and this lack of development leads to other concerns in reading, such as poor comprehension, lack of confidence in reading, and lack of interest in reading. Readers who are not fluent not only suffer from poor comprehension, but they also see themselves as unsuccessful readers and view reading as an unenjoyable task to be avoided whenever possible. One of the primary goals for these students is to develop some degree of fluency that allows them to move on to addressing the other concerns. Tier 3 instruction, then, is intended for individuals or small groups of students who exhibit significant difficulties in reading fluency that are impacting other areas of reading.

> *Readers who are not fluent not only suffer from poor comprehension, but they also see themselves as unsuccessful readers and view reading as an unenjoyable task to be avoided whenever possible. One of the primary goals for these students is to develop some degree of fluency that allows them to move on to addressing the other concerns.*

Our goal in writing this book is that you will be better able to make instructional decisions that are most appropriate to your students' instructional needs. Please keep in mind, however, that there is a great deal of flexibility in how you choose, modify, and implement the instructional models we provide. Any instructional lesson can be modified for work with individual students and larger groups of students. Moreover, we hope that the lessons and their components will empower you to develop your own models of fluency instruction in order to meet the specific needs of your students.

Fluency is indeed a critical component of proficiency in reading. And yet, it is too often neglected or misunderstood. We hope that the following chapters will allow you to make fluency a major goal of your own reading curriculum and, as such, help all of your students move to higher levels of overall proficiency and satisfaction in reading.

CHAPTER 1:

ASSESSMENTS

This book is based on the dual notions that reading fluency is a critical competency in learning to read and that there are various forms and tiers of fluency instruction available to teachers based on their students' needs. In order to know the level of instruction optimal for individual and groups of students, it is necessary to be able to assess students' level of fluency development (Rasinski, 2004). In this chapter, we describe simple yet valid methods for assessing fluency.

Before we get into the actual assessment of fluency, let's briefly review some basic principles of reading assessment. We do this because many of the assessments used in reading today are problematic in that they do not adhere to these important principles. First, reading assessments should be valid. That is, they should involve actual and authentic reading on the part of the student. Some assessments do not look like real reading. For example, in some assessments, students may be asked to read a list of nonsense words. This, to us, is not an authentic reading task. Second, reading assessments should be sensitive enough to detect changes in students' reading after relatively short periods of instruction or intervention. Having to wait six months before detecting whether or not an instructional intervention is working is too long. A good assessment should be able to detect changes in reading in two to three weeks. Third, reading assessments should be relatively quick to administer. Time given to assessment is time taken away from teaching. There exist many fine assessments of reading. Unfortunately, many of them require an hour or more to administer and another 20–30 minutes to score and interpret. Few teachers have that sort of time to devote to assessment, especially when they are working with 20 or more students. Although there are other characteristics of good reading assessments, we feel that the three we describe here—validity, sensitivity, and efficiency—are critical to making assessment work for our students.

> ... *reading assessments should be sensitive enough to detect changes in students' reading after relatively short periods of instruction or intervention.*

In the Introduction, we describe fluency as having two major components—proficiency in word recognition and proficiency in expressive reading. We then broke down word recognition into two subcomponents—accuracy and automaticity in word recognition. In the following sections, we describe simple ways to assess and monitor students' fluency development in these areas.

Accuracy in Word Recognition

Accuracy in word recognition refers to the student's ability to decode words, or to provide the oral pronunciation for written words. Clearly, accuracy in word recognition is an essential competency. For years, there has been a simple method for assessing accuracy in word recognition—simply determining the percentage of words a student reads correctly on a grade-level passage. Here is the protocol in a few easy steps.

1. Find a grade-level passage of about 150–200 words in length. If you are using a commercial reading program, you can use a passage from that program. Alternatively, you can find a passage from another source and apply a readability formula to it to ensure that it is at the appropriate grade level. (Try the Free Readability Text Consensus Tool on the Readability Formulas website for a no-cost text readability calculator.)

2. Make two copies of the passage: one for the student to read and one for you to mark.

3. Ask the student to read the passage aloud in his or her normal reading voice.

4. Mark any uncorrected word recognition errors that the student makes while reading. Also, mark any words that the student omits and requires assistance with from you.

5. At the end of the reading, remove the passage and ask the student to retell what he or she read.

6. When the student is not present, determine the percentage of words read correctly. You can do this by subtracting the marked errors from the total words in the passage and then dividing by the total number of words in the passage.

7. For all grade levels, students who are on grade level in terms of accuracy in word recognition should be able to read within 92 percent to 98 percent of the words in the passage correctly. Scores above 98 percent indicate strength in accuracy in word recognition while scores below 92 percent indicate that accuracy in word recognition may be a concern and require additional instruction or intervention.

Automaticity in Word Recognition

As we mentioned earlier, accuracy in word recognition is important for reading; however, it is not enough. Fluent, proficient readers need to be automatic or effortless in their word decoding. Automaticity in word recognition is best measured through reading speed. As readers become more automatic in recognizing words in text, they will naturally become faster in their reading. It takes less time to automatically recognize words than to have to stop and analyze the words that are encountered when reading. So simply checking reading speed is a good way to assess automaticity in word recognition. One problem that complicates things is that as students' move through the grade levels, their reading rates increase, so we have to examine each student's reading rate according to the grade level to which he or she is assigned. But here's the good part: Automaticity in word recognition can be assessed while testing for accuracy in word recognition. It simply takes a few additional steps:

1. When the reader begins to read the grade-level passage you have selected for accuracy in word recognition (see above), use a stopwatch.

2. At the end of 60 seconds, mark where the student is in the text.

3. Count the number of words the student was able to read correctly in that 60-second period. This gives you a "Words Correct Per Minute" (WCPM) score.

4. Check the student's WCPM score against Figure 1 to determine what tier of fluency instruction is most appropriate for the student.

FIGURE 1 Automaticity in Word Recognition: Tiers in Words Correct Per Minute for Midyear

Grade	Tier 1	Tier 2	Tier 3
1	>20	10–20	<10
2	>60	30–60	<30
3	>80	50–80	<50
4	>100	70–100	<70
5	>115	80–115	<80
6	>130	90–130	<90

The WCPM scores in Figure 1 are midyear (January) estimates based on Hasbrouck and Tindal's (2006) norms and our own work with students experiencing difficulty in fluency. If you assess students at times other than the middle of the school year, simply adjust the norms accordingly. For example, if you were to assess a second-grade student in October, you could estimate Tier 1 WCPM at >50, Tier 2 at 20–50 WCPM, and Tier 3 at <20 WCPM. Keep in mind also that these norms should be interpreted with some degree of caution. Use your own observations of your students' reading as well as other relevant data to make a final determination of the appropriate tier for fluency.

We wish to make one more important comment before moving on from automaticity. Although reading speed is an indicator of automaticity in word recognition, teaching children to read as fast as possible is not an appropriate way to teach or nurture automatic word recognition. Like any activity that can be automatized, automaticity in word recognition is best developed through authentic practice (reading, in this case). The fluency lessons described in this book provide you with approaches for developing this important fluency component.

Expression—Prosody

Oral reading with good expression is the second major component of reading fluency. Fluent readers and speakers use their voices to express and enhance the meaning of the text they are reading or speaking. The easiest way to assess expression is to simply listen to students read and rate their reading according to a rubric or rating scale. We have provided the Multidimensional Fluency Scale as a guide in Figure 2. Your assessment of expression can occur while students read for accuracy and automaticity. The steps appear below.

1. Remind students before reading the grade-level passage that you want them to read in an expressive manner.

2. Listen carefully to your students' reading. You may wish to record their reading for later analysis. Then rate them according to the four dimensions of oral reading: volume and expression, phrasing, smoothness, and pacing.

3. Each dimension can be rated from 1 to 4, so total scores can range from 4 to 16. Scores of 12 are indicative of students for whom Tier 1 instruction is best suited. Scores of 8 through 11 suggest Tier 2 instruction as most appropriate, and total scores of 7 and below suggest Tier 3 instruction.

4. For students who fall into the Tier 2 or 3 categories, you can examine ratings more closely to determine if one or more of the four dimensions were particularly problematic for these students.

FIGURE 2 Multidimensional Fluency Scale

Name _____

Use the following scale to rate reader fluency on the dimensions of expression and volume, phrasing, smoothness, and pace. Scores range from 4 to 16. Generally, scores below 8 indicate that fluency may be a concern. Scores of 8 or above indicate that the student is making good progress in fluency.

Dimension	1	2	3	4
Expression and Volume	Reads with little expression or enthusiasm in voice. Reads words as if to get them out. Little sense of trying to make text sound like natural language. Tends to read in a quiet voice.	Some expression. Begins to use voice to make text sound like natural language in some areas of the text but not others. Focus remains largely on saying the words. Still reads in a quiet voice.	Sounds like natural language throughout the better part of the passage. Occasionally slips into expressionless reading. Voice volume is generally appropriate throughout the text.	Reads with good expression and enthusiasm throughout the text. Sounds like natural language. The reader is able to vary expression and volume to match his/her interpretation of the passage.
Phrasing	Monotonic with little sense of phrase boundaries, frequent word-by-word reading.	Frequent two- and three-word phrases giving the impression of choppy reading; improper stress and intonation that fail to mark ends of sentences and clauses.	Mixture of run-ons, mid-sentence pauses for breaths, and possibly some choppiness; reasonable stress/intonation.	Generally well phrased, mostly in clause and sentence units, with adequate attention to expression.
Smoothness	Frequent extended pauses, hesitations, false starts, sound-outs, repetitions, and/or multiple attempts.	Several extended pauses, hesitations, etc. are more frequent and disruptive.	Occasional breaks in smoothness caused by difficulties with specific words and/or structures.	Generally smooth reading with some breaks, but word and structure difficulties are resolved quickly, usually through self-correction.
Pacing (during sections of minimal disruption)	Slow and laborious.	Moderately slow.	Uneven mixture of fast and slow reading.	Consistently conversational.

Score _____   (Adapted from Zutell and Rasinski, 1991)

Making Assessment Work for You and Your Students

As you can see, by having your students read one passage, you can assess all components of reading fluency. Keep in mind that assessment should not be used to place students in a tier or type of instruction. It should be used to monitor students' progress and to see if they are responding to the instruction you are providing. With that in mind, we suggest that once you have placed your students in a particular tier for instruction as well as found a particular lesson to employ, regularly check the progress they are making in fluency. For Tier 1 students, you might check every three months; for Tier 2, once a month may be appropriate; and for Tier 3 students, those students who appear to have significant difficulties in fluency, assessing progress every other week would seem most reasonable.

If during these monitoring assessments you find students making progress, continue to provide the instruction that seems to be effective. If, on the other hand, progress does not seem to be forthcoming, you need to reassess and perhaps change the instruction you are providing. Note also that you can use your regular assessments to move students to higher tiers of instruction if they demonstrate improved levels of fluency and overall reading proficiency.

> Note also that you can use your regular assessments to move students to higher tiers of instruction if they demonstrate improved levels of fluency and overall reading proficiency.

If the students you are assessing are frustrated as they read a grade-level passage, use the same assessment protocol with passages that are at a lower grade level. Keep in mind, however, that you will need to adjust your analyses and your use of the norms to account for student reading material that is lower than the assigned grade level. And when doing follow-up monitoring assessments, you will want to use material that is at the same level of difficulty as your initial assessment in order to make an apples-to-apples comparison.

Comprehension Matters

Although this chapter deals with assessment of reading fluency, we need to keep in mind that reading comprehension is always the ultimate goal of reading. Reading fluency is closely connected to comprehension. Students who are fluent readers tend to be good comprehenders. However, it is sometimes the case in which you have students who demonstrate difficulties in one or more components of fluency yet have good comprehension of the texts they read. We know that fluency is important for reading comprehension but not completely sufficient. So sometimes students might read in a choppy manner but still get the overall meaning. These students do indeed need help in becoming more fluent readers. However, additional instruction or intervention in fluency should not preclude students from reading materials they understand, even if those materials may be above the level indicated by their reading fluency. Both fluency and comprehension need to be addressed at their appropriate levels.

Conclusion

Reading fluency is only important to the extent that we can measure it. With the simple tools provided in this chapter, you should be able to identify strengths and weaknesses in the components of reading fluency, monitor progress in fluency, and make strategic instructional decisions to benefit students. Another benefit to the assessment protocol presented is that the results can easily be communicated to parents and students. Students who struggle in reading often do not see themselves making progress because they continually compare their reading to their classmates. The data you obtain from the assessment protocol in this chapter can demonstrate to students that they are indeed making tangible progress in their development to becoming proficient and fluent readers.

CHAPTER 2:

TIER 1 WHOLE GROUP FLUENCY INSTRUCTION

Reading fluency is a competency that all students must acquire in order to become proficient and meaningful readers. Ideally, fluency should be fostered as early as possible in students' reading careers and in large group or whole-class situations to enhance its effectiveness. Fortunately, many reading fluency activities lend themselves very well to whole-class environments at any grade level. Moreover, many of the fluency activities we will share in this section can easily cross into other content areas, such as social studies, science, music, and more.

Through large group fluency instruction, we provide students with an effective model of what fluent reading looks like and sounds like. We also involve students in activities in which they use fluent reading for real and engaging purposes, such as performing for an audience or participating in communal oral reading experiences. When such activities are made a regular and consistent part of the reading curriculum, large group fluency instruction can go a long way to developing fluency in all readers and helping students find great joy in reading.

The read-aloud is an activity that permeates the classroom lives of many children around the world. It is often done as a way to develop a love of reading and increase exposure to wonderful books that students may enjoy reading on their own. Read-alouds, however, can also serve an additional purpose. Teachers can use it to model for students what reading fluency is and how it can enhance the reading experience and improve comprehension.

Other large group activities involve the performance of a text (poem, song, script, or other work) for an audience. If students know they will be performing a reading selection, they will rehearse their reading in order to provide a listening audience with a satisfying and meaningful experience. Moreover, when students rehearse texts that will eventually be performed, they can focus on rehearsing an expressive reading that reflects and adds to the meaning of the text.

Round robin reading is an oral reading activity in which students are called on by their teacher to orally read portions of an assigned text. Although frowned on by literacy scholars as it violates several principles of good reading instruction, it continues to be a common practice in schools. Radio reading transforms round robin reading into an authentic and purposeful fluency-building activity that focuses students' attention on meaning, not turn taking. In radio reading, students are assigned parts after reading the entire text and then perform their parts as if on a radio program.

Many of the large group activities that we describe in this section are activities that many teachers are already familiar with and, in some cases, already implement in their classrooms. However, they may be used more for creating fun and engaging reading experiences for students and less for improving students' reading fluency as well as their understanding of fluency and its importance. With some minor tweaking, we hope to demonstrate that these activities, which are already part and parcel of your reading curriculum, can become powerful tools to moving students toward higher levels of reading fluency and overall reading proficiency. Moreover, we hope you will discover how the activities we present can easily move beyond the reading curriculum and make your content-area instruction more vibrant and effective.

> *With some minor tweaking, we hope to demonstrate that these activities, which are already part and parcel of your reading curriculum, can become powerful tools to moving students toward higher levels of reading fluency and overall reading proficiency.*

Reading Aloud

Many commercial programs for teaching reading fluency tend to over-emphasize reading quickly. Fast reading is associated with automatic word recognition, an important component of reading fluency. With this constant focus on reading speed, students can easily begin to view fast reading as a primary goal for reading. We have seen students read through passages as fast as they can during fluency instruction. When we ask them what they recall about their reading, they have little to say.

Fast reading without comprehension is not fluency. Fluency is reading at an appropriate pace and with good expression that reflects the meaning of the passage. Students need to develop an understanding of just what fluency is: meaningful reading. One way to show students fluent reading is to model fluent reading for them. When students see their teacher reading in a fluent and meaningful manner, they can attempt to emulate their teacher's fluency. Since most teachers already read aloud to their students, read-aloud time can be a chance to not only share a good story but also to demonstrate fluent reading for students.

Background

Read-aloud, quite simply, is a rather brief period of time (5 to 15 minutes) during the school day in which the teacher reads a favorite story or other text to students. This is often a favorite time of the school day for both students and teacher as the class can relax while listening to a great story. It is not unusual to see a noisy classroom reduced to a hush as students are captured by an engaging tale.

Although the read-aloud is viewed as a favorite and fun activity, there are good instructional reasons to read to students every day (Rasinski, 2010). First, the read-aloud is enjoyable. We know that motivation for reading declines as students progress through the grades. We're not sure why this happens, but we do know that read-alouds can be an effective antidote to this reading motivation problem. It is not uncommon to see students choosing to read a book written by the same author of a book read to them by their teacher. Read-alouds also affect students' comprehension. During read-alouds, the students' only job is to comprehend the passage read by the teacher. Because students do not have the added burden of having to decode the words, they can actually comprehend texts that are above their own reading level. Listening to more challenging texts will definitely lead to better comprehension. Read-alouds also increase student vocabularies.

When listening to texts that are above their own reading level, students will be exposed to more sophisticated words. Presented in a rich and meaningful context, those words are likely to be added to students' vocabularies that, in turn, will lead to improvements in their reading comprehension and written compositions.

> *During read-alouds, the students' only job is to comprehend the passage read by the teacher. Because students do not have the added burden of having to decode the words, they can actually comprehend texts that are above their own reading level.*

Teacher read-alouds do one more thing. They provide students with a first-hand model of what fluent reading is. Students hear their teacher adding meaning and enjoyment to the text that is being read through the use of his or her voice. Students can then internalize this model of fluent reading and work to make their own reading like their teacher's.

Materials and Procedures

The teacher read-aloud should be a daily activity. Reading a book to students will usually require several read-aloud sessions. Avoid spacing the read-aloud sessions too far apart from one another as students may lose track of the story. Having a special and nonnegotiable time of each day for read-alouds demonstrates the importance of the activity and creates anticipation on the part of the students.

The materials used for the teacher read-aloud should be books and other texts that the teacher wishes to share with students. Texts that lend themselves to oral expressive reading tend to work best. These texts often contain dialogue and episodes of varied types and degrees of emotional intensity. They work well because the teacher can use her voice to reflect and add to the meaning and tone of the text. Poetry, songs, and famous speeches also work well as these texts are meant to be read aloud with good phrasing and expression (or with melody in the case of songs).

Although there are no specific steps for read-aloud, there are certain tips that will make it an effective fluency activity.

- Rehearse the text you will be reading to students. By looking over and actually reading the read-aloud passage in advance, you will be able to plan your reading—what parts to read louder or softer, which parts to read fast or slow, where to place dramatic pauses, what words to emphasize, etc.

- Set the stage for the read-aloud. Make the read-aloud a special experience for you and your students by creating a mood. Dim the classroom lights a bit, and sit on a special stool. Allow students to gather on the floor in front of you or sit in comfortable chairs throughout the room. Periodically remind students that you expect them to be attentive listeners during this time.

- Use the time after the read-aloud to talk about the text and about your reading of the text. This helps cement students' understanding of the text and explore different interpretations of the text. The time after the read-aloud can also be used to talk about fluency with your students. Help students notice what you did with your voice to make the read-aloud experience more enjoyable and meaningful. Read back sections of the passage. Ask them to notice and respond to how you employed your voice to add meaning to those passages. Of course, make the point that when they read they should also attempt to use their voice, in both oral and silent reading, to reflect and add to the meaning of the passage.

> *Use the time after the read-aloud to talk about the text and about your reading of the text. This helps cement students' understanding of the text and explore different interpretations of the text.*

Adaptations

Students can get a better grasp of what fluent reading is by hearing negative examples. Occasionally beginning a read-aloud in a slow, halting, word-by-word manner will get a curious look from students. At that point you can stop and discuss what was happening. Did the students enjoy the reading in this fashion? Did they find it more difficult to pay attention and understand what was being read? Of course, the answers are the reading was neither enjoyable nor easy to understand. The take-away for students is if they do not enjoy or easily understand text when it is read to them in a slow and halting manner, they need to try to avoid reading in that manner.

On other occasions, you may wish to read excessively fast, with multiple mispronunciations or with multiple regressions where, after reading a portion of a sentence, you regress back to the beginning. These and other readings with poor fluency demonstrate to students what they should avoid in their own reading. When modeling disfluent reading, keep such readings brief and always be sure to reread those sections in a more fluent manner. We certainly don't want students fixating on poor and disfluent reading.

Lower Elementary Grade Example

Mrs. Barclay has been teaching first grade for close to 20 years. "I absolutely love teaching these beginning readers, and my favorite activity is to read to them daily … sometimes more than once in a given day. My students need to be exposed to good books as soon as possible in order to get hooked on reading." Mrs. Barclay's main intent on reading aloud is not to focus on fluency. However, she has noticed that in order for her to read in a way that her students enjoy, she needs to read through or rehearse the text in advance.

"I have a chart in my room that lists the characteristics of good reading," she tells us. The chart has expression, loudness, pacing, and posture listed. "Often, after I read to my students, we will evaluate my reading according to the chart. I'd much rather have students evaluate me, especially if I may have not read well, which sometimes happens, than have them evaluate one another. I'm tough; I can take the criticism."

Upper Elementary Grade Example

In Mr. Epperley's third-grade class, the tables are sometimes turned. "Of course I read to my students as often as I can, and I try to do so with as good expression as possible. But I also want my students to develop into fluent readers themselves. So when they give an oral book talk about something they recently read, I ask them not only to talk about the book, but also to choose a short section and read it to the class." By requiring students to read a text aloud, students have to search for sections of their text that lend themselves to expressive oral reading. "Then I remind them that they need to practice reading their passage before reading it to the class. Sometimes it is pretty evident students forgot or chose not to rehearse. Those are good times for me to have a personal chat with that student about the need to look it over in advance."

By allowing students the opportunity to engage in a read-aloud, Mr. Epperley is helping students develop a sensitivity to the elements of texts that require fluent reading. He has also noticed that the process of rehearsing and performing a read-aloud develops students' confidence in themselves as fluent readers. Mr. Epperley calls it "stage presence."

> *By allowing students the opportunity to engage in a read-aloud, Mr. Epperley is helping students develop a sensitivity to the elements of texts that require fluent reading.*

Effectiveness

The goal of the read-aloud is to help students develop a greater awareness of the nature, purpose, and need for fluent reading. In order to become fluent, one needs to know what constitutes fluency. The proof that the read-aloud accomplishes this goal is best found in the comments we have heard over and over again from teachers who use read-alouds to develop greater awareness of reading fluency. Perhaps Mrs. Barclay puts it best when she says, "I love how our discussions on my fluency evolve over the year. At first they are not sure what to say, but after several weeks they become quite precise in their comments on my reading. Then, when I confer with them individually, they will often use that same fluency-related language to talk about their own reading. Clearly, they know what it means to be a fluent reader."

Poetry Slams

This performance-based fluency activity provides students with the opportunity to rehearse and recite poetry for an audience. During this strategy, students choose a new poem each week and practice accurate and expressive reading in order to prepare for the big poetry performance. On Fridays, students engage in the poetry slam—dressed in black and with the lights down low in an attempt to create a coffeehouse environment.

Background

Like many reading fluency strategies, poetry slams rely on the research-based foundation of repeated readings (Kuhn & Stahl, 2003; National Institute of Child Health and Human Development, 2000). We know that the more students practice reading, the better they become. Practice in reading also prepares them for the higher-level texts they will encounter in the future (Samuels, 1979). In an authentic twist to repeated readings, we select a text that further supports fluency development. Poetry is unique because it is written to be performed, making it an ideal genre for fluency development (Young & Nageldinger, 2014). Because the performance is judged mostly on the reader's expression, rehearsing and reciting poetry also emphasizes an often-neglected fluency goal: prosody (Wilfong, 2008).

> *In an authentic twist to repeated readings, we select a text that further supports fluency development. Poetry is unique because it is written to be performed, making it an ideal genre for fluency development* (Young & Nageldinger, 2014).

Materials and Procedures

For a poetry slam, you will need plenty of poetry. Make sure to highlight various types of poetry from a range of time periods. Providing ample choices for students is imperative for student engagement.

You may want to begin this weekly activity after a poetry unit so students already have preferences and an understanding of and an appreciation for poetry. After building their background knowledge, you can begin the poetry slam framework, which can continue throughout the year. Similar to our reader's theater example, we created a five-day format. We dedicate only five minutes per day to rehearsal, but we make sure students have enough time to reread their poems at least three times per day.

DAY ONE: Students choose a poem based on their interest and/or poetic preferences. These can be from poetry books in the classroom, the library, or collections found online. Students take the poem home and ask a family member to read it aloud.

DAY TWO: Students highlight difficult words and ask their peers or you to help with word identification. The goal of the day is to make sure the students can read every word accurately. Then students bring the poem home and read it aloud to someone (or something).

DAY THREE: Students practice reading with expression, paying close attention to the author's intended meaning. This includes reading by chunking the text purposefully, which means paying attention to the phrases that should be read together.

DAY FOUR: Students pair up and practice reading to each other. During the five-minute rehearsal, they are encouraged to coach one another as necessary.

DAY FIVE: It is finally time for the poetry slam. We encourage students to wear all black to school. We also use dim lamplight. In the front of the classroom, there is a single stool and possibly a café table. Each student recites his or her poem for the class, and the audience "snap claps" to show appreciation.

Lower Elementary Grade Example

The lower grades example follows the five-day format, but the level of teacher support increases. Ms. Pearce is a second-grade teacher who has weekly poetry slams. She follows the format, but she pays close attention to the selection of poems. Although she believes that students can potentially, with enough practice, master any poem, she does not want them to be frustrated. Therefore, on poem selection day, she might direct students away from long complicated poems. On day two, Ms. Pearce roves the classroom, listening carefully for students who might need assistance. She wants to make sure every student knows each word. It may be that she meets one-on-one with a student or perhaps calls a small group together to work on some of the tricky words. On day three, Ms. Pearce might actually read some of the students' poems aloud to them, thus serving as a model for fluent poetry reading. On day four, similar to day two, she roves the classroom and listens intently for any potential issues. She wants to make sure that every student, regardless of assessed ability, can stand confidently before their peers and expressively recite their chosen poems.

Upper Elementary Grade Example

Down the hall in a fifth-grade classroom, Mr. Hernandez implements poetry slams a bit differently. He uses the five-day format, but he encourages students to choose challenging poems. He believes the harder, the better. After all, his fifth graders have four days to rehearse, at least three reread-ings per day, and the opportunity to practice at home. That's a minimum of 12 rehearsals, which Mr. Hernandez observed to be sufficient. On day two, students sometimes look up words in the dictionary or online. It is not enough to recognize the complex words in the poems; students also need to know what they mean. Understanding the vocabulary will support students' overall comprehension of the poem, which will also help them match their expression with the meaning of the poem. Mr. Hernandez emphasizes comprehension on day three, making sure students understand the meaning of the poems—a necessary process to enhance the final performance. A stronger focus on comprehension sets this day apart from the second graders down the hall. Although the second graders do analyze the poems for meaning, the fifth graders select much more sophisticated poems, requiring a much higher level of analysis. But, in the end, they are all dressed in black, reciting poetry slams in their classroom coffeehouse.

Adaptations

For students who demonstrate "stage fright," consider allowing groups of students to perform a single poem. You could do this for a few weeks until students are more confident and the stage fright dissipates. For students who struggle, we recommend that you meet with those students and use one of the Tier 3 interventions. We believe that Read Two Impress (see page 80 in Chapter 4) would be a good first choice. The method has a strong assisted reading component but also allows for independent practice. Finally, poetry is universal and poems are available in all languages; therefore, you might allow bilingual students to choose poems in their native language.

Effectiveness

Poetry slams used in this way have a similar effectiveness as reader's theater, which has a strong research base promoting its use (Griffith & Rasinski; 2004; Martinez, Roser & Strecker, 1998; Young & Rasinski, 2009). Wilfong (2008) used a variation of poetry slams and found that students' reading rates, word reading accuracy, and comprehension increased. In addition to these important reading processes, students' attitudes toward reading in school also improved. Thus, poetry slams can promote fluency and increase students' motivation.

> *Wilfong (2008) used a variation of poetry slams and found that students' reading rates, word reading accuracy, and comprehension increased.*

Speeches

Speeches are recommended for fluency practice as they are meant to be read aloud and can be rehearsed easily. When using speeches for fluency practice, students must first understand the purpose of the speech. Once they understand its purpose, they are better able to embed expressive elements in their delivery that enhance the speech's overall impact.

Background

Rehearsing speeches offers a wonderful and authentic reason to repeatedly read text aloud. Thus, when students rehearse speeches, they also focus on the prosodic component of fluency (Zutell & Rasinski, 1991). In addition, the experience is more authentic because there is a performance.

Materials and Procedures

You can find a plethora of speeches on the Internet, including those written centuries ago by Socrates or more contemporary State of the Union addresses. Students can also write their own speeches. You or your students can search for "famous speeches," "historical speeches," or "contemporary speeches"—as you can see, the possibilities are endless. A note about Internet research: For Internet safety reasons, you may want to conduct this research before class time and suggest a few speeches that will be appropriate for your class.

The following procedures are not necessarily steps, but guidelines to teach your students and to consider as a teacher. The focal point of rehearsal should be on prosody, and thus students need a good understanding of prosody's components. Prosody includes reading expression, volume, phrasing, smoothness, and pace. We will use the Multidimensional Fluency Scale (MFS) (Zutell & Rasinski, 1991) to help develop a clearer understanding of how students can use the prosodic elements to refine their speeches.

First, students need to consider expression and volume. Your students need to experiment with varied expression that matches the purpose and meaning of the speech. They should also consider an effective variation of volume that increases the speech's impact. When a speaker lowers his or her voice, it engages the crowd differently than increasing volume. Lower volume captures the crowd and fosters anticipation, while a louder voice may serve to dramatize or emphasize main points, conveying importance to the audience.

Speeches are typically smooth and intentionally phrased. Speakers do this, as with most of the expressive elements, for effect. Speakers may also pause to emphasize points. So your students need to experiment with phrasing and consider potential parts of the speech where intentional pausing would enhance their delivery. In the end, it is important that students read smoothly, with good phrasing, and of course, with purposeful pausing.

Finally, students should calibrate the pace of the speech. This is an important tool that speakers use during the delivery of their speeches. Slowing down to add emphasis and speeding up to capture the attention of the audience are powerful adjustments that can significantly enhance the effectiveness of a speech. During rehearsal, help your students locate parts of the speech where the varying of pace could increase the speech's impact. Also help your students identify the prosodic adjustments and explore the intentions behind their expressive choices. Many times you can find the actual recorded speech online that students choose, especially more contemporary speeches. These recordings can serve as a model for students' rehearsals. Though we do not have a particular format for rehearsal and performance, you might use the five-day format we presented for poetry slams. Of course, you may vary the format based on the complexity and length of speeches that students choose. We will present potential frameworks for both primary and intermediate students below, but as always, these frameworks are flexible and we encourage you to change them to meet your students' needs.

Lower Elementary Grade Example

Ms. Degaish budgets two weeks for each speech cycle. During week one, she asks her third graders to write their own speeches. Sometimes she asks them to choose nonfiction topics, such as how to play certain sports, how to eat healthy, or descriptions of animals that students researched. Other times, she asks them to research historical figures and write speeches from their perspective. For example, one student wrote a speech about hitting home runs as if he were Babe Ruth. However, in this example, Ms. Degaish asked students to write a fun, fictional speech titled, "If I Were King of the World."

Using the writer's workshop model, students spent the first week writing their speeches. They engaged in planning, drafting, revising, editing, and conferring with the teacher. After completing the writing process and refining their final drafts, they spent the second week rehearsing their speeches. Ms. Degaish requires three days of rehearsals, and she splits the speech performances on the final two days of the week. Because there are many speeches and her students are young, she wants to make sure that they can sit, pay attention, and be respectful to each speaker. Dividing the performances between two days reduces the time students have to sit and listen.

On the first day of week two, the students meet in small groups and take turns explaining the purpose of their speeches. In this case, the main point is the same: to explain what they would do as king of the world. After explaining their purpose, the students read aloud their speeches to themselves to make sure their point is made and their purpose is evident.

The second day of rehearsal begins with an analysis of their speeches to embed expressive elements. To scaffold and support students, Ms. Degaish supplies a checklist (see below) of elements for students to consider while rereading and planning their speech delivery. Students are also provided with highlighters to mark some of the prosodic features on their speech.

Speech Checklist

☐ I need to read the entire speech fluently, and it should sound like natural speech.

☐ I can raise my voice when something is very important. (highlight yellow)

☐ I can read quietly when I want the audience to listen carefully. (highlight green)

☐ I can pause when I want the audience to think about what I just said or get them excited about what I am going to say next. (mark with an "X")

☐ I can read faster when I am building up my main point. (highlight orange)

☐ I can read slower when I am reading about really important points. (highlight pink)

On the third day, Ms. Degaish's students reread their speeches to themselves, attending to their prosodic markings. After a few rehearsals, the students pair up, and partners take turns reading their speeches to each other. Partners provide feedback about each other's delivery. This serves as their final practice before their speech delivery. Ms. Degaish asks students to self-assess their readiness and encourages those in need of more practice to take their speeches home and practice with someone or rehearse in the mirror. On the next day, half of the students perform their speeches for the class, and the other half delivers their speeches on the following day.

Upper Elementary Grade Example

Mr. Ricard teaches fifth grade and uses a rotating schedule for speeches. Each week, five students are required to choose speeches that match the content of the lessons. Because he has 25 students, each student is required to choose, rehearse, and deliver a speech every five weeks. He leaves the choice open to interpretation and encourages creative or literal connections. A more literal connection might be delivering Ronald Reagan's speech regarding the *Challenger* space shuttle disaster when studying about the solar system. However, a more creative connection might be demonstrated when studying fact and opinion and a student chooses to deliver Barbara Jordan's statement on the articles of impeachment. Though it is a complicated speech, the student has ample time to practice. The student may also choose to read sections rather than the entire speech.

At the beginning of the week, the five students choose their own speech and inform Mr. Ricard of their choices. He then approves or asks students to keep searching. He is careful to make sure speeches are appropriate and that students will be able to master the speech with only a week's worth of practice. After final approval, students take their speeches home and engage in the weekly rehearsal process. Mr. Ricard provides the students with these guidelines for practice.

DAY ONE
- Accurately recognize all of the words.
- Know the meanings of all words.
- Know the overall meaning of the speech.
- Understand why the speech was written and who it was written for.
- Reread the speech three times.

DAY TWO
- Analyze the speech for the following:
  — Places to increase/decrease volume,
  — Words to emphasize with expression,
  — Places to speed up or slow down, and
  — Places to pause.

- Reread the speech two times, experimenting with expression, volume, emphasis, pace, and pauses.
- Make a final decision on expression, volume, emphasis, pace, and pauses.
- Reread the speech one more time after making these final decisions.

DAY THREE
- Rehearse the speech in the mirror.
- Reread the speech three times.

DAY FOUR
- Rehearse the speech twice for two different people (at home or at school).

DAY FIVE
- Deliver the speech to the class.

After each speech, Mr. Ricard engages the classroom in a discussion about the overall meaning of the speech and how it connects to their learning. He then explains the upcoming learning objectives and selects the next five students who will deliver speeches the following week. The students can spend some time over the weekend perusing speeches online to identify a speech that connects to the week's learning objectives. He repeats this cycle for the entire year, so each student typically delivers seven speeches throughout the year.

Adaptations

For an alternative model, the students can rehearse their speeches and upload audio or video recordings of their speeches online. Instruct students to watch them for homework. For an added incentive, ask students to vote for their five favorite speech deliveries. You can then view the top five in class and hold an anonymous vote on the "speech of the week." This speech could then be entered into a "speech of the year" contest. Having a discussion about what makes the speech stand out could inform students' upcoming speech preparations. For students who find the process difficult, you can help them find shorter speeches that are less challenging. There are many speeches online just for kids (check out Pinterest). Other sites provide speech topics specifically for students in the lower elementary grades, so they can write their own.

Effectiveness

We believe that speeches are ideal for fluency development (Young & Nageldinger, 2014). Three strong principles make this method effective and engaging. First, repeated readings promote fluent reading (National Institute of Child Health and Human Development, 2000; Samuels, 2002). Second, the focus on meaning and expressive reading requires students to think carefully about the purpose of the speech and how to adjust their prosody to increase the impact of the delivery (Rasinski, 2010; Young & Nageldinger, 2014; Zutell & Rasinski, 1991). Third, rehearsing for an actual performance adds authenticity—an element that motivates students to practice and do their best.

> *... the focus on meaning and expressive reading requires students to think carefully about the purpose of the speech and how to adjust their prosody to increase the impact of the delivery*

Reader's Theater

Reader's theater is a fun, engaging, and effective way to increase students' reading fluency (Griffith & Rasinski; 2004; Young & Rasinski, 2009) and motivate young readers (Martinez, Roser & Strecker, 1998). We define reader's theater as groups of students who dramatically read a text for an audience. Students spend a week rehearsing their scripts in groups to prepare for performance. The performance does not require costumes or props; students entertain audiences with their expressive oral reading.

Background

We know that repeated readings are an effective method to increase reading fluency (Kuhn & Stahl, 2003; National Institute of Child Health and Human Development, 2000; Samuels, 1979). Tyler and Chard (2000) described reader's theater as a natural link to repeated readings. While reader's theater includes opportunities to reread, it also provides an authentic reason for doing so—the performance. According to Martinez, Roser, and Strecker (1998), repeated readings in the context of reader's theater motivated young readers, a notion confirmed by Rinehart in 1999. The authentic and motivational aspects make the strategy ideal for simultaneously promoting fluency and a love for reading.

> *While reader's theater includes opportunities to reread, it also provides an authentic reason for doing so—the performance.*

Materials and Procedures

To implement reader's theater in your classroom, all you will need are scripts and highlighters. The Internet is a great resource, and you can locate scripts by searching for "reader's theater scripts." You can also create your own. You can take any text and rewrite it in script form by adding narrators and/or characters. You can also easily transform poetry into scripts by simply adding narrators (see Figure 3 for an example).

FIGURE 3 **Poetry-to-Script Conversion Example**

Poem	Script
Roses are red.	Reader 1
Violets are blue.	Reader 2
Bacon is tasty.	Reader 3
And easy to chew.	All

Next, decide on a format that works best for your classroom. We typically use a five-day format (Young, 2013) and dedicate 5 to 10 minutes per day to reader's theater, but you can adjust this to meet the needs of your students and schedule.

DAY ONE: Read a few scripts aloud, and ask students to think about which script they might want to select for the week. Then students choose a script and read it for the overall meaning. If the students find it difficult to read, they can read it chorally, or one student in the group can read it aloud. After the reading, send the scripts home and tell students to read it again while thinking about which part they might like to play.

DAY TWO: On this day, students engage in the part selection process. Yes, we know what you are thinking—and yes, in the beginning it can be somewhat chaotic. But think back to your childhood and the many creative ways you used to settle disputes. Does "Rock, Paper, Scissors" come to mind? If more than one student is adamant about playing a particular role, a quick game of "Rock, Paper, Scissors" (or any other method you choose) works splendidly. Once every student in each group has a role, the students highlight their parts and begin the first read-through. Because this is the first reading practice, students focus mainly on word recognition. We make sure students know all of the words by encouraging them to practice and ask for help when encountering a difficult word. After 5 to 10 minutes, students put their scripts in take-home folders and practice again when they get home.

DAY THREE: The third day's focus is on expressive oral reading. At this point, students should have a good understanding of the text, which will help them read aloud with an expression that matches the meaning. With the aid of teacher and peer coaching, students practice their lines while attending to volume, expression, phrasing, smoothness, and pace. Students practice for 5 to 10 minutes. The reason we suggest a time limit rather than a number of repeated readings is because the length of scripts differs from group to group, and groups may not finish at the same time. Having a time limit helps avoid the dreaded question, "What do I do now?"

DAY FOUR: Students engage in a practice performance. This is when students stand and pretend they are performing. During the practice, students make sure they are reading accurately and expressively and get feedback or assistance from the teacher. The students take the scripts home again for one last practice. For short weeks, this day can also serve as performance day.

DAY FIVE: It is finally performance day. The students have practiced and they are ready. It is important to secure an audience to keep the activity motivating and authentic. We like to invite parents, administrators, and other school staff. You can also take your show on the road to other classes or the front office. If audiences are scarce, the groups can perform for each other.

Lower Elementary Grade Example

Mr. Kent uses reader's theater in his second-grade classroom. For this week, he decided to convert humorous children's poetry into scripts. He has a class of 24 students, so he prepares six scripts, each containing four parts. Mr. Kent believes his kids work more effectively in smaller groups, so he prepares more scripts to keep the group numbers low. Plus, if he cannot locate an audience for performance day, the groups can perform for each other.

He reads the scripts aloud and asks student to think about which script they want. After reading them, he holds up each script and asks, "Who wants to be in this one?" Hands shoot up, and he passes out the scripts. In one case, a student was unable to be in a desired group because of the limited number of parts. He explains to the student that she will have plenty of opportunities to get the scripts she wants; after all, reader's theater lasts all year, leaving 35 more chances! Of course, you can handle this situation however you see fit.

Students return to their seats and read over the script, then place it in their take-home folder for their nightly practice. On the following day, students enter the classroom and immediately get out their scripts. In Mr. Kent's classroom, rehearsals take place first thing in the morning. Students sit with their groups and begin the part-selection process. After some debate and a few rounds of "Rock, Paper, Scissors," the students raise their hands to indicate the process is complete. Before giving the groups highlighters, Mr. Kent double-checks the selection process. He does this by first asking who plays each part, making sure each part is accounted for and that no two (or more) students believe they have the same part. Once Mr. Kent is satisfied, he gives each student in the group a highlighter to highlight his or her part. He instructs his students to read through their script as many times as possible in five minutes and to focus mainly on pronouncing the words.

Students arrive on the third day, get their scripts, and practice for five minutes. Mr. Kent instructs students to focus on reading expressively, providing assistance when necessary. During practice on day four, he asks students to practice as if they were performing. He walks around the room and listens to each group to make sure they are ready. Mr. Kent notices that one student is still having difficulty with word recognition and expression. He makes a note of this and plans to meet with the student one-on-one later in the day. There are several interventions that might help the student become more accurate and expressive, and Mr. Kent chooses to use the Neurological Impress Method (NIM) (Heckelman, 1969), a technique in which the teacher and student sit side by side and read a text together, with the teacher reading slightly ahead of the student. A description of NIM can be found in Chapter 4 on page 73. After 15 minutes of one-on-one NIM tutoring, the student is able to read the text accurately and expressively.

However, to make sure the student is fully prepared, he plans to use NIM with the student one more time before the performance. He knows it is important for students to read confidently on performance day so that even struggling readers can read alongside their peers with precision.

Previously, Mr. Kent invited his principal and two first-grade classes to attend the performances. As the honored guests arrive, they find their seats, eagerly awaiting the humorous performances. Because of the extensive practice, every student is adequately prepared to entertain the audience with their expressive oral readings. Mr. Kent joins the audience and sits back to bask in his students' fluent oral readings.

Upper Elementary Grade Example

Mrs. Zang is a fifth-grade teacher who consistently implements reader's theater. She uses a variety of different texts, including excerpts from novels, classic poetry, and lots of nonfiction. This week, Mrs. Zang chose five nonfiction scripts about important historical figures. Although there are five groups, not all of the groups are equal in number because of the predetermined number of parts in the scripts. She had to purposefully choose scripts to make sure all 28 of her students had a part. Because the scripts are relatively long, she chose not to read them aloud, but she briefly summarized each historical figure to help students make informed decisions about their scripts. As with the lower grades example, Mrs. Zang follows the five-day format and asks that students read over their entire script to determine which role they might like play.

On the second day, students return with their scripts and keep them available until their afternoon practice. Mrs. Zang's class rehearses their scripts after recess. She prefers this time because it allows for an easy transition from playtime to instruction. She makes sure all students have selected parts and then passes out highlighters. Students engage in the first reading making sure they know all of the words. They do this independently but are encouraged to seek help from the teacher or peers if they encounter new or complex words. She also places an emphasis on the meanings of content-specific words, roving the classroom and listening for important vocabulary in order to provide explanations for her students.

On day three, the students focus on expressive reading. She roves the classroom again to make sure that students' expression matches the meaning of the text, and she coaches when necessary. After the 10-minute rehearsal, students place their scripts in their backpacks and take them home to practice reading expressively. The following day, students practice the performance in groups in preparation for performance day. On performance day, the students take their show on the road and perform for several third-grade classes. Through conversations with the third-grade team, Mrs. Zang found out that third graders were writing biographies on historical figures and that the performances were both entertaining and informative.

Adaptations

Reader's theater is easily adapted for any grade level by adjusting text difficulty and interest. Reader's theater research indicates that it is effective in primary (Young & Rasinski, 2009), intermediate (Griffith & Rasinski, 2004), and secondary classrooms (Keehn, Harmon & Shoho, 2008). In addition, the activity can be integrated across the curriculum. For example, you can find nonfiction scripts online about a variety of topics, such as the water cycle, state history, animal adaptations, the digestive system (fun!), and mathematical concepts like division. Students can also become a source for scripts. You can lead your students through the complex process of scripting using mentor texts, creating parodies, or turning their own writing into scripts (Young & Rasinski, 2011).

> In addition, the activity can be integrated across the curriculum. For example, you can find nonfiction scripts online about a variety of topics, such as the water cycle, state history, animal adaptations, the digestive system (fun!), and mathematical concepts like division.

Effectiveness

We (Young & Rasinski, 2009) implemented reader's theater with second graders over the course of the school year, and the results indicated that students doubled the expected growth in reading rate, increased reading expressiveness by 20 percent, and improved their reading comprehension.

Griffith and Rasinski (2004) implemented reader's theater with fourth-grade students and saw remarkable growth. Many of the students who were previously at risk read on grade level by the end of the year, and some demonstrated nearly two years of reading growth. In addition to reading growth, students became more motivated and confident readers (Martinez, Roser & Strecker, 1998; Rinehart, 1999).

> *Griffith and Rasinski (2004) implemented reader's theater with fourth-grade students and saw remarkable growth. Many of the students who were previously at risk read on grade level by the end of the year, and some demonstrated nearly two years of reading growth.*

Rock and Read

Rock and Read is a reading fluency activity that is proven to enhance volume, expression, and pace (Young, Valadez & Gandara, 2016). Essentially, the students participate in karaoke in the classroom. It is a fun and engaging way to promote fluency while reading (Iwasaki, Rasinski, Yildirim & Zimmerman, 2013).

Background

Listening while reading is a timeless fluency strategy that was first studied by Chomsky in 1976. In her study, five 8-year-old children read along with audio books for four months, and all made significant gains in reading fluency and overall reading achievement. Since then, educators and researchers derived many reading fluency strategies based on the premise that audio-assisted reading can enhance reading fluency (Kuhn & Stahl, 2003). Iwasaki, Rasinski, Yildirim, and Zimmerman (2013) reported on an instructional method whereby students learned one or two songs each week while tracking the words as they sang. During the school year, all but one student made at least a year's growth, and many students exceeded the average reading growth expected in a single school year. Researchers reported that the students were motivated to sing by performing for others.

> *... educators and researchers derived many reading fluency strategies based on the premise that audio-assisted reading can enhance reading fluency* (Kuhn & Stahl, 2003).

Materials and Procedures

For this activity, the materials and procedures differ slightly among the lower and upper grades, but the general steps are very similar. We will make this clear here and in subsequent scenarios. First, you need to identify which songs you want your students to learn and perform. This will vary by grade level, interest, and to some degree, teacher preference. Of course, you want songs to be appropriate for school but also engaging or, dare we say, popular. Thus, we will not stipulate which songs to choose, but we only recommend you consider the songs carefully before introducing them to your students. We recommend you choose two songs per week. You can set the practice schedule however it best suits your needs and the needs of the students. For example, you can practice both songs daily and hold the performance on Friday. Or you can have students practice one song for two days, perform the song, and then practice another song for two days and hold another performance. We do not recommend that you practice one song for the entire week because our goal for the students is not to memorize the song, but to read along. We summarize these steps in the list below.

1. Identify two songs that students will practice and perform.

2. Practice the first song for two days.

   a. For younger students, we recommend that you print the lyrics and project them while pointing to the words. This allows you to guide the students and adjust the pace, stopping when necessary to provide support.

   b. For older students, you can use the multitude of karaoke songs found online (i.e., YouTube). Simply search for any song, followed by the term "karaoke" or "karaoke version." Of course, you may see that your students would benefit more from the model mentioned above. Similarly, if your younger students are ready, you can also use the karaoke model.

3. Perform the song for each other or invite audiences that might include other classes, school staff, or parents. Remember, you can always take your show on the road, too!

4. Repeat with the second song for the second half of the week. Note: Older students might be able to learn two songs at the same time and perform both at the end of the week.

5. Continue this weekly format for the remainder of the school year.

> *Perform the song for each other, or invite audiences that might include other classes, school staff, or parents. Remember, you can always take your show on the road, too!*

Lower Elementary Grades Example

Mrs. Power decides that Rock and Read might be a good way to help students develop their reading fluency. Because Fridays are usually dedicated to buddy reading and the enjoyment of texts, she believes that a four-day format works best for her classroom. In addition, there are several four-day weeks, and she wants to make sure to implement Rock and Read consistently and without interruptions. She drafts a schedule that looks like this:

DAY ONE: Introduce new song and practice

DAY TWO: Practice and perform

DAY THREE: Introduce new song and practice

DAY FOUR: Practice and perform

Then Mrs. Power considers the details and activities of each day. Here is how it plays out after she meticulously plans the daily routines. For the first song, she chooses "Learning to Fly" by Tom Petty. It has a lot of repeated phrases, and the vocabulary is not too difficult. On day one, Mrs. Power introduces the song and plays it for the students. After listening to the song, she projects the lyrics so students can see them. Pointing to each word, she engages students in a choral reading. After the reading, she points out any tricky phrases or difficult words and then does one more choral reading. After the two readings, she plays the song, invites students to sing along, and points to the words throughout the text. After completing the first rehearsal, she invites them to sing along one more time. For day one, the students listened to the song, read it twice, and sang along twice.

On day two, she prints the lyrics for the students and reads through the song once. Then she and the students sing the song twice. So the rehearsal on day two consists of one reading and two sing-alongs. Mrs. Power decides that the students are ready for the performance. She scheduled a performance for a first-grade class down the hall. She knows that an audience is an important motivator for students and gives an authentic purpose for rehearsal. Equipped with their own copy of the lyrics, students travel to the first-grade classroom and sing their hearts out.

Mrs. Power repeats the process for the next two days with a new song. She chooses "Roar" by Katy Perry. It is longer than "Learning to Fly," but she knows that students love the song. On day three, she introduces the song, plays it for the students, projects the lyrics, guides students through two readings, and has one singing rehearsal. On day four, she gives students their own copy of the lyrics and guides them through one choral reading and two singing rehearsals. On this performance day, Mrs. Power invites parents to the classroom to listen to their young vocalists. It is a great opportunity to involve parents as well as showcase her class of fluent readers.

Upper Elementary Grade Example

A fourth-grade teacher, Mr. Pearce, feels that his students could benefit from Rock and Read, tailors it for older students. Mr. Pearce believes that having two performances may take too much time away from other instruction, so he decides that students will perform both songs on Fridays. He believes that students can learn and practice two songs per day. His schedule looks like this:

DAY ONE: Introduce and practice songs one and two

DAY TWO: Practice both songs

DAY THREE: Practice both songs

DAY FOUR: Practice both songs

DAY FIVE: Performance

In preparation, Mr. Pearce searches the Internet for karaoke videos and selects two songs that students will rehearse throughout the week. On day one, he plays an original version of the song for students. Next, he plays the karaoke video with the sound off. Students read along without singing the song to familiarize themselves with the lyrics. Then Mr. Pearce turns up the audio and students sing along two times. He repeats the process with the second song.

Over the next three days, students practice each song once per day. Mr. Pearce feels that rehearsing each song more than once per day may be somewhat monotonous. On performance day, Mr. Pearce invites the parents to the classroom to listen to their young vocalists. He views it as a great opportunity to involve the parents as well as showcase his class of fluent readers.

Adaptations

If you teach upper elementary, you can use the lower-grades example if students need more support throughout the rehearsal process. Conversely, if your lower-grade students are competently working through the process, you can switch to the upper-grades example. In addition, Rock and Read works in any language. All you need are the lyrics. You can also add a writing element by asking students to write parodies of the songs used during Rock and Read. It is a complex creation process that requires students to think critically about the intended meaning of the original song and how it can be modified to be more humorous. Because Rock and Read only uses the music, students could perform their parodies in groups or as a class.

Effectiveness

Young, Valadez, and Gandara (2016) found that consistent use of Rock and Read in the classroom positively impacts students' reading fluency. Fifty-one second graders participated in the study and engaged in a total of 240 minutes of Rock and Read. In just four weeks, Rock and Read significantly increased students' ability in volume, expression, and pacing. It also improved students' reading rate, but this was also true for the control group, which engaged in the regular reading curriculum. Thus, it appears that teachers are readily equipped to increase students' reading rate; however, it is also important to use strategies that increase the expressive aspects of reading fluency.

Choral Reading

Choral reading is a classic method for developing students' reading fluency. Along with the teacher, the class reads aloud the same text orally. You can use this strategy with any text on a daily basis.

Background

Despite research on the effectiveness of choral reading in upper elementary grades, Rasinski (2010) mentions that most choral reading takes place in the primary grades and is less common in the upper grades. We encourage you to implement choral reading regardless of grade level. Reviews of fluency research indicate choral reading is a viable means for fluency development at all elementary grade levels (Kuhn & Stahl, 2003; National Institute of Child Health and Human Development, 2000). There are many variations of choral reading, but the simple definition is reading aloud as a group (Vacca, Vacca & Gove, 2000).

Materials and Procedures

All you need is a text that everyone can see and a group of students. Our procedure follows a gradual release model. In the beginning, the teacher has much of the responsibility and then slowly places the responsibility on the students.

1. Display the text or give copies of the text to each student.

2. The teacher reads the text aloud.

3. Students and the teacher read aloud together.

4. Students read aloud without support of the teacher.

Lower Elementary Grade Example

In Mrs. Bruun's second-grade class, students begin each day with a choral reading. After the morning announcements, her students gather on the carpet in front of the projector. She likes to use poetry because the students enjoy it and she believes that poetry is structurally suited for fluency instruction. (Fluency researchers agree.) She first reads the poem aloud and points to each word while her students listen and follow along. Next, she asks students to join in for the second reading—the choral reading of the poem. Finally, she places all of the responsibility on the students and they read the poem aloud together without her support. So the students listen to the poem while reading along, chorally read with the support of the teacher, and chorally read while the teacher listens.

Upper Elementary Grade Example

Mr. Griffith, a fifth-grade teacher, uses the same structure as Mrs. Bruun, but he only requires choral reading three times per week—mostly because he chooses longer and more difficult texts. Mr. Griffith also makes sure the selected text aligns with the current unit of study. For example, when studying the American Revolution, he selects *Paul Revere's Ride* by Henry Wadsworth Longfellow as the text for choral reading. He first reads the entire poem to the students. He reads seriously, with good volume and great expression. For the second reading, he invites his students to join him and encourages them to pay close attention to the words as well as expression. After the students and teacher chorally read, he prepares students for their choral reading without the support of the teacher. Mr. Griffith tells students that their choral reading is like performing for their teacher. He wants his students to get into it and read with enthusiasm and expression. The entire process takes a bit longer because of the complexity and length of the text, but Mr. Griffith realizes that fluency is also a concern for intermediate grades.

Adaptations

There are many ways to conduct choral reading in the classroom. You could use the provided format above, or you could adapt it to fit the needs of your students or text selection. For example, you might read the text aloud three times together. Or you may want to read it aloud with half of the class the first time and the other half the second time. In another variation, you might read the text aloud once, ask students to rehearse in groups, and then return to the meeting place to chorally read as a class. Though these modifications are slight, sometimes novelty promotes student engagement.

Effectiveness

Choral reading is an effective reading strategy that promotes fluent oral reading (Rasinski & Padak, 2004). In addition, choral reading is a great way to encourage your English language learners (ELLs) to engage in oral reading practice. Because everyone is reading aloud together, ELLs may feel more comfortable reading aloud (McCauly & McCauly, 1992). Overall, the strategy helps develop automatic readings so students can then focus more of their attention on reading comprehension (LaBerge & Samuels, 1974).

Conclusion

This chapter described several research-based activities to use with your entire class. Not only do these strategies help develop reading fluency, but they can also increase overall reading achievement and motivation. We know that you cannot implement all of these activities every day, so we encourage you to choose one or two you like the most. If used consistently, each of the activities should sufficiently develop reading fluency for many of your students. Although these methods have strong research support, some of your students may require more intense fluency instruction. In the next chapter, we describe Tier 2 strategies that are more intense and offered in small group contexts, which may benefit those students who did not respond to Tier 1 instruction.

CHAPTER 3:

TIER 2 SMALL GROUP READING FLUENCY INSTRUCTION

If your students are demonstrating difficulties with fluency despite Tier 1 fluency instruction, you might consider delivering Tier 2 interventions to a small group of students who could benefit from more intense fluency instruction. In this section, we offer several research-based methods that are best delivered in a small group setting for those students who need that additional fluency boost. We recommend that you meet with your Tier 2 groups often, perhaps two to three times per week or more.

First, you will read about echo reading. The teacher conducts echo reading in small groups. This method is for students who need extra scaffolding and the opportunity for immediate practice. Echo reading is a type of gradual release that helps students independently read aloud difficult texts with accuracy and expression, thereby also boosting confidence.

Next, we describe paired reading, an approach that does not necessarily require the teacher to meet with the student—all you need to do is pair a more fluent reader with a less fluent reader. It could be an older student, a parent, or another volunteer. It is an engaging approach that allows for choice and builds on social relationships, giving more attention to the student in need of intervention. Essentially, it is a variation of choral reading aimed at increasing accuracy, rate, and expressive reading.

For a more holistic approach, we describe a guided reading delivery method that emphasizes objectives in accuracy, fluency, and comprehension, which is ideal for teaching other literacy skills along with fluency. Finally, we conclude this chapter with the Fluency Development Lesson, a framework that you can use with small groups daily to build their reading fluency.

Echo Reading

Echo reading is a fluency-building technique whereby a teacher reads a sentence aloud to a small group of students. Then the students echo, or reread, the same sentence aloud while focusing on accuracy and prosody. The echoing continues for the entirety of the text.

Background

This method is derived from listening-while-reading strategies (Chomsky, 1976). While Chomsky only asked students to listen while reading, this strategy entails a teacher reading a sentence aloud while students listen and then repeat it back to the teacher. So then, it differs from traditional listen-while-reading strategies in that students first listen and then read. Therefore, this strategy has an added gradual release component in which the teacher models the reading and students have an immediate opportunity to practice.

Materials and Procedures

This strategy calls for an independent-level text and a small, homogeneous group of readers. You can use your existing guided reading groups, but instead of selecting an instructional-level text, choose one that students can read easily. Then again, we always recommend that you stretch your lessons to your students' highest potential, so you might consider an instructional-level text or perhaps even a frustrational-level one.

Next, make sure each student in the group has a copy of the text. Explain the procedure in kid-friendly language:

1. I will read a sentence out loud.

2. You will listen carefully to the words and my expression.

3. Then you will all read the sentence out loud to me.

4. Read aloud with good expression.

Begin the procedure by reading aloud. Make sure the students listen carefully, and then echo read with accuracy and expression. Continue this for the entire book, passage, or poem.

Lower Elementary Grade Example

In Mr. Nash's second-grade classroom, groups engage in echo reading once per week. He uses his existing guided reading groups and picks one day per week to switch his instructional method to echo reading. For example, one of his groups is reading at a beginning-of-second-grade level, about a half-year behind the expectation. Because of the added support that echo reading provides, he chooses a level 24 (midyear second grade) book in hopes of rapidly increasing students' reading abilities. Mr. Nash obtains five copies of *The Team* by Sally Murphy, one for himself and one for each of the four students in the group. He begins by explaining the procedure. "Today we are going to do some echo reading. I will read a sentence aloud and then you will all read the same sentence back to me. Listen carefully to how I read with expression, and do your best to read it aloud like I did. This book is called *The Team*. Let's start with chapter one." Mr. Nash then reads the first sentence aloud:

Mr. Nash: "'Catch!' called Kelly, as she threw the basketball to her friend, Mischa."

Students: "'Catch!' called Kelly, as she threw the basketball to her friend, Mischa."

Mr. Nash listens for accuracy and expression. If he does not hear it, he might read it aloud again, and point out the specifics of his expression. Mr. Nash says, "See that exclamation mark? That means we read the word 'catch' enthusiastically. Try it with me."

Mr. Nash: "Catch!" (reads loudly and emphatically)

Students: "Catch!" (also read loudly and emphatically)

Mr. Nash is satisfied, and he observes his students as they read the text. The quick reteach on the word "Catch" helped his students see exactly what Mr. Nash was looking for. He and the group continue echo reading. The goal is to read either the rest of the text or read it for the next 15 to 20 minutes, whichever comes first.

Upper Elementary Grade Example

A group of fourth graders are reading considerably below grade level in Mrs. Valadez's class. The group of students struggles greatly with fluency and requires considerable scaffolding when tackling difficult texts. In order to adhere to RTI-based recommendations that students requiring Tier 2 interventions should receive at least 60 minutes of small group instruction per week (National Center on Response to Intervention, 2010), Mrs. Valadez has dedicated three days per week to a group of six struggling readers and provides echo reading for approximately 20 minutes. She believes the strategy is perfect because the gradual release model and teacher support provide the necessary scaffolding that her students need. They are currently studying savannas, so Mrs. Valadez chose to use *Wild Savanna Zoos* by Lucinda Cotter, a second-grade book that is at the instructional level of her group of students.

She begins by explaining the procedures to the group. "I am going to read this book sentence by sentence. You will reread each sentence aloud after I've read it to you. Make sure you read it like I did—with good expression." She begins by reading aloud the first heading.

Mrs. Valadez: "What Is a Savanna?"

Students: "What Is a Savanna?"

Mrs. Valadez listens carefully to make sure the students mimic her expression. Because the first heading is in the form of a question, she makes sure that students read it as such with the proper inflection. Once she is satisfied, she continues the echo reading procedure for the next 20 minutes. It is possible she will need an additional text, depending on the length.

Adaptations

The easiest way to modify echo reading is to adjust the text difficulty. If you find that your students struggle, decrease the level of the text. Conversely, if they appear to engage in the strategy with ease, perhaps it is time to increase the level of the text. You can also modify the strategy to fit the chosen text type. For example, if you choose to use poetry, you may not want to read each sentence (if it even has sentences), so you could read line by line or perhaps short stanzas.

Effectiveness

Researchers have studied the effectiveness of echo reading and found the method to be a powerful way to increase students' reading fluency (Homan, Klesius & Hite, 1993). Echo reading can potentially increase reading accuracy, rate, and expression (Rasinski, 2010). However, it must be implemented consistently to achieve the desired results. Thus, if you choose to use echo reading with your students, find a good place for it in your schedule and stick to it.

Paired Reading

Paired reading is a great way to develop fluency. However, some students may need a more direct and intense form of assisted fluency instruction. Paired reading provides students with a one-on-one experience in assisted reading. As the name implies, a less fluent reader is matched with a more fluent reader. For a regular and specified period of time, usually 10 to 20 minutes, the two readers read together chorally and simultaneously. The more fluent reader adjusts his or her voice to keep pace with the less fluent reader.

Background

Although the procedure seems simple enough, the results can be quite impressive. Through a number of studies on paired reading, Keith Topping (1987a, 1987b, 1989, 1995) found that daily use of paired reading with struggling readers can make dramatic improvements, not only in students' reading word recognition and fluency, but also in their reading comprehension and overall reading achievement.

Materials and Procedures

The beauty of paired reading is that it can be used with any text. Normally the student who is being tutored (tutee) chooses the text—it can be pleasure reading, assigned reading by the teacher, or perhaps even incidental reading, such as something found in a magazine. By allowing the tutored student a choice, we are giving him or her ownership of the activity. The material should be at the tutee's instructional level—challenging but not frustrating (usually this means material at which the tutee can read about 95 percent of the words correctly).

> *By allowing the tutored student a choice, we are giving him or her ownership of the activity.*

The procedure is also easy to implement. The tutee and his or her partner (tutor) sit comfortably side by side. On cue, the tutee and tutor read the text orally. Note: Paired reading does not involve the readers alternating lines or paragraphs—both readers read the same text together or chorally. As the reading continues, the tutee follows along by pointing to the words in the text as the pair reads. The tutor adjusts the rate of his or her reading to that of the tutee and the difficulty level of the passage; however, the tutor may wish to slightly "push" or "pull" the tutee by reading at a slightly faster clip than the tutee. Also, if the text or a portion of the text is more challenging than usual, the tutor can also read in a slightly louder-than-normal voice to provide more support to the tutee.

If the tutee feels comfortable and confident enough to "go solo," or read without the assistance of the tutor, he or she can signal the tutor with a tap on the wrist or some other nonverbal cue. When such a signal is given, the tutor simply stops reading aloud but continues to read silently. When the tutee signals again, that is the tutor's sign to continue reading aloud with his or her partner.

If the tutee makes a word-decoding error when paired reading with the tutor or alone, the tutor simply states the correct pronunciation of the word while pointing to it and signals the tutee to do the same. There is no need to stop and make a lesson out of a word-decoding error. That would take away from the authentic reading experience and divert both readers' attention from the meaning of the passage. The tutor can make a mental note of any errors made during the paired reading and chat about them with the tutee at the end of the session. A brief discussion about the text and the tutee's reading usually concludes a paired reading session.

Adaptations

What we like about paired reading is that it is an authentic reading experience. The student who is the tutee chooses the text and has some control in the intervention, perhaps then increasing the engagement factor. The essence of paired reading is simply two readers reading (and enjoying) a text together. There are many ways that paired reading can be varied in order to create a variety of reading experiences.

First, the person playing the role of the tutor can change. It can be the teacher, a parent, another family member, a classroom volunteer or aide, an older student, or a classmate. The main consideration is that the tutor needs to be a more fluent reader than the tutee. As mentioned earlier, the text that is used in paired reading can change depending on the preference of the tutee. However, if the tutor finds a particularly intriguing text for paired reading, there is no reason why he or she cannot recommend a text or series of texts for paired reading.

Repeated reading is a highly regarded approach for fluency development. Paired reading can easily be matched with repeated reading in order to get a synergistic effect. A text read one day can be reread on a second day (perhaps with the tutor providing somewhat less support, such as reading in a softer voice and allowing the tutee's voice to lead the reading). After the second (and perhaps even a third) day of reading a text, the tutor and tutee should discuss how the tutee's reading has improved. It's very encouraging for the tutee to see that the amount of text read in a 10-minute period increased from the first to second (and even third) reading. An added benefit is that the improved fluency from one reading to the next allowed the tutee to cover more text.

> *Repeated reading is a highly regarded approach for fluency development. Paired reading can easily be matched with repeated reading in order to get a synergistic effect.*

We think it is a good idea to spend a few minutes talking about the tutee's reading after a paired reading session. The tutor should focus on the positive aspects of the tutee's reading—confident voice, good expression, pausing at appropriate points, good phrasing, etc. The tutor may also bring up some areas for improvement. If word recognition errors seem to plague the paired reading, the tutor may wish to spend a bit of time focusing on the errors, providing the tutee with strategies for working through difficult words and also talking about the meaning of such words.

Lower Elementary Grade Example

Second-grade teacher Mrs. Robinson thinks that students should read as much as possible. So, in addition to encouraging reading in school, she works hard to get parents and families involved in students' reading. "I love that my parents read to their children daily. It's perhaps the most important thing that they can do, and I remind parents about it all the time." Mrs. Robinson thinks that parents can do even more at this critical stage in their students' reading. Early in the school year, she asks parents to attend one of several hour-long sessions on paired reading. During the training, she describes paired reading, demonstrates how it is done with a student, and asks parents to practice with their own children. Then she asks parents to do paired reading with their children at least three times a week. She provides parents with a weekly log to track their paired reading with their children.

"The improvement, especially in my struggling readers, is quite remarkable." Mrs. Robinson is so sold on paired reading that she regularly sends home notes and has paired reading trainings and follow-ups throughout the school year. In fact, every May she celebrates her students' and parents' success with a paired reading celebration in her classroom. It's at that time that she asks parents to sign a pledge to continue to do paired reading during the summer break.

Upper Elementary Grade Example

Like many classrooms around the country Ms. Destin's fifth-grade class contains high, average, and struggling readers. While sustained silent independent reading is a daily occurrence in her classroom, Ms. Destin also adds variety into her class's reading experience with paired reading activities. Every other month she will pair her stronger readers with students who are less fluent. Then for 10 to 15 minutes, the pairs of students find a quiet corner or area of the classroom and engage in paired reading. Some months, she assigns one book that she thinks students would enjoy reading in this manner. Other months, she allows each reading pair to choose a text.

"No question, paired reading is well worth the time I take to train students in doing it. What I really like about my way of doing paired reading is that it encourages students to help one another. Even the more advanced readers seem to benefit as they develop empathy and provide support for their partners. I will often match partners who may not normally be 'best buddies.' Yet it is so neat to see them work together to read and understand a book or other text."

Later in the year, Ms. Destin will work with a third-grade teacher and allow volunteers to engage in paired reading with third-grade partners. Ms. Destin notes that this allows her struggling readers to read texts that they can more easily master and puts them in the position of being the helper as opposed to the student who is receiving the help. "It truly is a win-win situation for all students involved!"

Guided Reading

Guided reading is a well-researched classroom-tested strategy for helping small, homogeneous groups develop their reading skills and proficiency (Fawson & Reutzel, 2000; Fountas & Pinnell, 1996; Goldenberg, 1992). The teacher groups three to five students based on their instructional reading levels and provides explicit instruction in various aspects of reading using appropriately leveled text. This is a great context for explicit fluency instruction.

Background

According to the gradual release of responsibility model, guided reading is the last step before independence. Teachers provide scaffolds but place much of the responsibility on the students (Pearson & Gallagher, 1983). The goal is to help students internalize reading processes, skills, and strategies they can eventually use independently. Thus, it is imperative that we offer students enough support for a successful reading of the text but not too much, which can make planning guided reading relatively difficult. Careful calibration of difficulty, wisely chosen objectives, and thoughtful planning are all necessary for a quality guided reading lesson.

> *According to the gradual release of responsibility model, guided reading is the last step before independence. Teachers provide scaffolds but place much of the responsibility on the students* (Pearson & Gallagher, 1983).

Materials and Procedures

First, the text should be at the students' instructional level. If the books are too easy or too difficult, students may not meet the lesson's objectives. Vigilant assessment is essential before grouping and text selection. It is imperative that students are grouped according to their respective reading levels. The assessment impacts the instruction and text selection, both of which should be targeting a common level. Once you select the text, read it. A reading of the text is crucial because it directly relates to how we choose the objectives. Next, choose the goals and execute the lesson, and finally, provide a follow-up lesson or reteach strategies.

Though there are many perspectives on the number of goals the guided reading lesson should meet, we like to choose three: one for comprehension, another for accuracy, and a third for fluency. The trick is that you have to match the goals with the content and level of the text as well as to students' needs. So how can we accomplish this? The following sections describe two scenarios. We walk you through text selection, choosing goals, and planning the lesson. Because of the focus on fluency, we will only mention the other goals briefly and spend more time on possible fluency objectives and follow-up lessons.

Lower Elementary Grade Example

We have a group of second graders reading at an instructional level L (midyear second grade). We select *Miss Nelson Is Missing!* by Harry Allard as our text and read it carefully, noting the features of the text that may support our goal selection process (Pinnell & Fountas, 2007). There are many options to consider for comprehension, but we feel the complex feelings that lead Miss Nelson to her decision to assume the disguise of the demanding substitute, Viola Swamp, should be analyzed. Thus, our comprehension goal is to infer the feelings and motivations of Miss Nelson. Before reading, we explain this goal and ask students to pay close attention to how Miss Nelson feels throughout the text and how these feelings impact her decisions. There is also a plethora of accuracy goals to work on with students reading this level L text, but we feel that solving multisyllabic words with inflectional endings and affixes might be a good goal. The word *misbehave* is conjugated in different ways, such as *misbehaved* and *misbehaving*. We can alert students to the root word, *behave*, and discuss the changed meaning when adding the prefix *mis–*. In addition, we discuss how to quickly and accurately decode words with different endings, such as *–ed* or *–ing*.

Finally, we select the fluency goal from several choices at this level. (See the list on the next page.) Considering the changes in characters and extensive dialogue in the story, we choose "Read dialogue with appropriate expression that reflects the voices of the characters." Coincidently, this goal directly relates to the comprehension goal because students need to first analyze the characters in order to properly read the dialogue as if they were the characters. We can make this connection explicit by explaining that a deep understanding of the characters and events in the story is necessary to achieve the fluency goal.

Possible fluency goals include:

- Read with good phrasing.
- Read with appropriate expression that matches the meaning of the text.
- Read dialogue with appropriate expression that reflects the voices of the characters.
- Adjust expression, volume, pitch, and tone; and demonstrate pausing to match punctuation.
- Read at an appropriate pace.

Now that we have our goals, we need to plan a few possible follow-up lessons. We typically relate these to the three goals, and so we plan three possible lessons aimed to extend or reteach the goals for comprehension, accuracy, and fluency. These are short lessons that should only take a few minutes. At the end of the lesson, we can determine which of the three to use based on our observations of student needs during the guided reading lesson. As noted previously, we will only describe a possible fluency extension or reteach. Assume that students did not attend to the changing voices of characters, and thus we employ the fluency follow-up lesson.

One possible lesson could be to engage the students in a mini reader's theater. We assign the students different roles, such as the kids, Miss Nelson, and Viola Swamp. First, describe and discuss what each of the different characters might sound like, noting different character traits. For example, for the role of the kids, we conclude that in the beginning of the story, the kids take on a naughty tone, later turn somewhat apprehensive, and finally experience feelings of relief. A discussion of how these feelings change will help students adjust their expression and use the appropriate voice. Next, knowledge of particular character traits also supports students' understanding of how the voices of Miss Nelson and Viola Swamp differ and how each might talk; Miss Nelson is sweet and gentle and Viola Swamp is likely the opposite. Once students understand the different voices, they can practice reading the dialogue as if they were the characters. Not only is this a great conversation and fluency practice opportunity, it is a lot of fun and students enjoy it.

Upper Elementary Grade Example

Suppose we have a group reading at an instructional level Q (beginning of fourth grade). *The True Story of the 3 Little Pigs!* by John Scieszka is a fun, fractured fairy tale at the students' instructional reading level. Like the previous example, we read the text and begin the goal selection process (Pinnell & Fountas, 2007). The story lends itself to many comprehension goals, but it is important to remember that the goals must also meet the needs of the students. By this level, students are likely making good predictions and connections or are able to identify standard story elements. So for this text, we choose a goal that asks students to evaluate the author's use of humor and how it adds to the enjoyment of the story. When considering accuracy, there are a lot of common words in this text, but there are a few unusual words as well. Therefore, we might designate "decode unusual words" as an accuracy goal. There's a lot of "huffing, puffing, and snuffing," and things get "jazzed" up; students need to read these unusual words accurately, which can be difficult because context does not always help with unusual or made-up words.

The author also uses lots of different types of punctuation and in ways that may be unfamiliar to students. For example, when the wolf introduces himself, the author uses short phrases broken by periods for effect. The author employs common punctuation like exclamation points and question marks as well as less common punctuation, such as hyphens and quotation marks, within dialogue to reference previous statements. Considering the range of punctuation usage, we believe that "demonstrate pausing to match punctuation" would be a good selection from the possible fluency goals listed below for this level.

Possible fluency goals include:

- Read with good phrasing.
- Read with appropriate expression that matches the meaning of the text.
- Read dialogue with appropriate expression that reflects the voices of the characters.
- Adjust expression, volume, pitch, and tone, and demonstrate pausing to match punctuation.
- Read at an appropriate pace.
- Use structural cues to apply stress on words.

- Use structural cues to adjust intonation.

- Attend to words in bold or italics, and read with appropriate expression.

- Reflect attention to various types of punctuation through oral reading.

The short follow-up lesson, again, directly relates to the fluency goal. In this case, we might have a little fun with punctuation. That is, we could change the punctuation in sections of the text and examine how the meaning and expression changes. For example, we can reparse the introduction of the wolf to "I'm the wolf and my name is Alexander T. Wolf, but you can call me Al." Removing the punctuation and rephrasing the text into one sentence changes the voice and author's intended effect. Students might discuss how this change takes away from the voice of the wolf—it might seem less matter-of-fact. In other places in the text, we changed the punctuation to a period instead of an exclamation mark. We can then discuss how this also changes the voice and meaning of the text. With a period, it almost makes the text more nonchalant. And just for fun, change it to a question mark to make the characters seem unsure of themselves. This follow-up lesson will help students understand that attention to punctuation is important for fluent reading and that authors intentionally use a range of punctuation and creative parsing to add voice to their writing.

Adaptations

Guided reading is a versatile instructional method than can be adapted for any group of students. Although most teachers group students homogeneously, heterogeneous groupings are also appropriate when the objective of the lesson is not necessarily on leveled reading behaviors but on other skills that a group of students may need (Cunningham, Hall & Sigmon, 2000). So if you have a group of students that have trouble with phrasing, regardless of their level, you can focus your lesson on developing that skill. However, it is important to choose a text that all of the students can read with assistance.

Effectiveness

Guided reading is an excellent venue for explicit instruction in reading processes, skills, strategies, and behaviors. Teachers who implement successful guided reading as a part of daily instruction see remarkable gains in their students' reading achievement (Ford & Opitz, 2008). Not only is the systematic instruction important for students' growth in reading, but the small group context provides students with much needed "teacher time," where students enjoy the undivided attention from their beloved teacher, which is, in our opinion, paramount for student success.

> *Not only is the systematic instruction important for students' growth in reading, but the small group context provides students with much needed "teacher time," where students enjoy the undivided attention from their beloved teacher, which is, in our opinion, paramount for student success.*

Fluency Development Lesson

Many students who struggle with fluency rarely get a chance to view themselves as successful and fluent readers. They read a text one time and feel they (and their classmates and teacher) realize they did not read the text well, certainly not nearly as well as their more advanced classmates. When this sort of mediocre reading happens on a daily basis, students can easily become discouraged and regard reading as a chore to be avoided as much as possible. Such an attitude guarantees that the students will continue to make minimal progress in reading.

The primary goal of the Fluency Development Lesson (FDL) is for less fluent students to achieve success in reading on a daily basis. When using the FDL daily, students will be able to read a new text fluently and meaningfully. Students will have concrete evidence of their ability to read texts well and make continual progress in their reading. This daily success will lead to even more reading and even more growth and success, which can lead to increased confidence.

Background

Literacy scholars have indicated that there are several approaches for successful fluency instruction. These include modeling fluent reading for students, providing students with assistance while reading, and repeated reading. Individually, these components will have a positive impact on students' fluency and overall reading achievement. But combined into a single lesson format, the components interact with one another to create a synergistic effect. The effects of a lesson that combines these components is greater than the sum of the effects of each component implemented individually.

The FDL takes a synergistic approach to fluency instruction. It integrates the components into a single, relatively brief lesson in which the goal is the fluent reading of a text that students could not read fluently at the beginning of the lesson.

Materials and Procedures

Ideally, the FDL should be implemented on a daily or near daily basis. The effects of one lesson will spill over to the next and so on. When implemented daily, students will pull themselves up by their own bootstraps to higher and higher levels of fluency.

The essential material for the FDL is a daily text. Because the lesson is relatively brief and the goal of the lesson is for students to read the text fluently, the text itself cannot be terribly long. We recommend a text of 50 to 200 words in length, depending on the difficulty of the text itself and the students' level of reading. We also suggest choosing a text that has a good sense of voice so that when students rehearse the text, their rehearsal is aimed at reading with expression and voice. Short segments from stories students have read in the past or will read in the future work well. However, we have found that rhythmical texts, such as poetry and song lyrics, work particularly well for the FDL. Poems and song lyrics are complete texts in themselves, are usually short, and are meant to be read aloud with good expression. The rhythm and rhyme embedded in poems and song lyrics make them enjoyable to read and also make them a bit easier to learn to read. So to do the FDL, you will need to find a new text for each lesson. If you choose to go with poetry, you will find many collections of poems for children of all ages simply by searching the Internet. For each lesson, make two copies of the poem for each student.

> *... we have found that rhythmical texts, such as poetry and song lyrics, work particularly well for the FDL. Poems and song lyrics are complete texts in themselves, are usually short, and are meant to be read aloud with good expression.*

The lesson itself takes about 15 to 25 minutes per day. It can be implemented within the reading instruction period or at a separate, special time during the school day. Here are the steps for implementing the FDL:

1. The teacher introduces a new short text and reads it to the students two or three times while the students follow along silently. The text can be a poem, segment from a basal passage, trade book selection, etc.

2. The teacher and students discuss the nature and content of the passage as well as the quality of the teacher's reading of the passage.

3. The teacher and students read the passage chorally several times. Antiphonal reading and other variations are used to create variety and maintain engagement.

4. The teacher organizes students into pairs or trios. Each student practices the passage three times while his or her partner or group listens and provides support and encouragement.

5. Individuals and groups of students perform their reading for the class or another audience, such as another class, a parent visitor, the school principal, or another teacher.

6. The students and their teacher then choose four to five interesting words from the text to add to the individual students' word banks and/or the classroom word wall.

7. Students engage in 5 to 10 minutes of word study activities (e.g., word sorts with word bank words, word walls, flash card practice, defining words, word games, etc.).

8. Students take a copy of the passage home to practice with parents and other family members.

9. The following day, students read the passage from the previous day to the teacher or a fellow student for accuracy and fluency. Words studied from the previous day are also read, reread, grouped, and sorted by individuals and groups of students. Students may also read the passage to the teacher or a partner who checks for fluency and accuracy.

10. The instructional routine begins again with step 1 using a new passage.

Lower Elementary Grade Example

Mrs. Horowitz knows that fluency is a foundational reading competency that her second-grade students must develop in order to move on to deeper levels of reading. She has adapted the FDL as a whole-class activity that she begins most days with. A daily nursery rhyme or song is posted on chart paper. "I find that most of my students are not familiar with nursery rhymes, so this is a great way to get them to discover and learn to read them at the same time." After each day's morning announcements, Mrs. Horowitz introduces the poem to students and reads it to the class using different voices. After a short discussion about the content of the poem and her readings, the class reads the text with Mrs. Horowitz and then continues practicing in small groups for 5 to 10 minutes.

Mrs. Horowitz has arranged for a different parent volunteer to be stationed outside her classroom each day of the week at about 9:00 a.m. Once students have rehearsed and mastered their poem, they are permitted to read their poem, individually or in small groups, to the classroom volunteer. The parents have been trained to provide assistance when needed and lavish the children with praise for their hard work. Mrs. Horowitz notes, "I can't believe that children will rehearse like they do to perform for an audience of one. The feedback from that parent volunteer is enough to make my children want to practice, practice, practice!"

The word study component of the FDL occurs in the afternoon so that Mrs. Horowitz can remind her students to continue reading their daily text at home to their parents. However, the brevity of the poem makes it easy for Mrs. Horowitz's class to continue to read it chorally throughout the day—before and after recess, before and after lunch, etc. According to Mrs. Horowitz, the daily text is the common thread that holds the day together. "We start and end each day with our daily poetry reading," she says.

Upper Elementary Grade Example

Mr. Snyder, a reading interventionist, works with third-, fourth-, and fifth-grade students. As with other reading teachers, he has found that most of his students struggle with word recognition and fluency. Since he has his students for only 30 minutes two to three days a week, he has to implement the lesson in its totality during this time period. He tries to implement the FDL at least twice a week. "These students simply are not fluent readers. And their lack of fluency is impacting their comprehension."

Mr. Snyder organizes his FDLs around poets. Over the course of several lessons, students will focus on the poetry of one particular poet. "We just finished Shel Silverstein. The kids loved his work! From Shel, we are going to move onto looking at the poetry of Langston Hughes. In my work with students, they get to read and read the poetry of a number of famous poets."

Mr. Snyder coordinates his work with the classroom teacher so that students also get opportunities to read the poems Mr. Snyder has selected in their own classrooms, as well as at home. Mr. Snyder requires his students to continue practicing their assigned poem at home with parents and family members.

Adaptations

The FDL can easily be adapted for a variety of instructional situations. It can be used in large groups, small groups, and even with individual students. Although we envision the FDL being implemented by a trained professional teacher or reading interventionist, it can be implemented by trained paraprofessionals, volunteers, and even parents and other family members at home. Indeed, *Fast Start* (Padak & Rasinski, 2005, 2008) is a home-implemented version of the FDL that has shown great promise in advancing the literacy progress of the most at-risk students (Rasinski & Stevenson, 2005). In *Fast Start*, the parent and child read a short selection together several times until the child is able to read it independently and perform it for the parent. The child's reading performance is followed by a brief examination or study of selected words from the text.

Since the FDL depends largely on a daily brief text and assisted reading, the lesson lends itself very well to a technology application. The daily text can be posted on a classroom website or e-mailed to students. A modeled reading of the text can also be posted or e-mailed to students. With these two items, students can listen to the text, read the text while listening to the fluent reading, and read the text independently any time they want. In addition, students can make a recording of the reading that can be sent back to the teacher. Word study can be practiced by way of a simple worksheet that can also be provided electronically to students.

Effectiveness

Since the FDL incorporates features that we know are elements of good fluency instruction, there is reason to believe that students who engage in it regularly will make good progress, not only in fluency but also in reading comprehension. We have used the FDL as the core lesson in the Kent State University Reading Clinic. Data from a recent study indicates that students make progress in fluency above and beyond even ambitious goals (Zimmerman, Rasinski & Melewski, 2013). Interestingly, the academic reading gains are often overshadowed by the gains in confidence made by students who previously did not view themselves as good readers or even readers at all. As one student told us after using the FDL regularly for five weeks of summer instruction, "I think I'm a better reader now!"

Conclusion

The goal of this chapter was to describe slightly more intense fluency methods for readers who demonstrate some difficulty. It is our sincere hope that at least one of these methods will be a good fit for your students who require Tier 2 instruction. We acknowledge that there is no one method best for every student or occasion, so we encourage you to evaluate the elements of each method to make an informed decision. You might even explain the possible interventions to the students and let them decide. Whether you choose echo reading, paired reading, guided reading, or the FDL, be consistent and evaluate your students' progress often. If you see little to no growth after consistent implementation of these methods, it might be time to consider a Tier 3 intervention.

CHAPTER 4:

TIER 3 ONE-ON-ONE READING FLUENCY INTERVENTIONS

Sometimes children need intense reading fluency interventions, and thus need Tier 3 interventions. If students do not respond to the whole group (Tier 1) or small group approaches (Tier 2), we recommend using one-on-one interventions. We realize that this takes time, but our experience confirms that these intense interventions have the potential to correct reading fluency difficulties when large group fluency instruction fails, and thus we believe this is well worth your time and effort. After all, it is our responsibility to make every child a competent reader who will enjoy the benefits of reading for a lifetime. These interventions take time but can potentially change a life forever. Fortunately, other capable adults, such as parents, paraprofessionals, university students, or other volunteers, can help deliver the recommendations in this chapter (Young, Mohr & Rasinski, 2015).

The following are fluency interventions that can support students who require Tier 3 support. The implementation varies and each emphasizes different constructs of reading fluency. In the first section, we discuss the method of repeated readings (Samuels, 1979). This method is the least assisted approach and has several implications we will discuss later. Regarding fluency development, the method emphasizes automaticity through practice and thus primarily enhances reading rate and accuracy in word recognition. Therefore, the method of repeated readings is ideal for students who read slowly, laboriously, or spend a great deal of cognitive energy decoding words.

We then describe what Heckelman (1969) called the Neurological Impress Method (NIM). Teachers offer more assistance to the reader with this method as it attends to several constructs of reading fluency, including word recognition, automaticity, and prosody. There is less concern with reading rate and more attention given to prosodic elements, such as phrasing, smoothness, and expression. The method is also more of a modeled approach rather than practice. As the tutor and child engage in NIM, the process helps the child unveil the unwritten laws of prosody while attempting to mimic adult-like reading. NIM is ideal for a reader who struggles with prosody and word recognition and, to a lesser extent, pace.

Flood, Lapp, and Fisher (2005) added a comprehension component to NIM, calling it NIM Plus. Keep in mind, however, that NIM Plus is almost identical to the original method, but the teacher *assesses* comprehension after the reading. We emphasize *assesses* because there is no actual comprehension instruction involved, rather questions at the end of the reading to be used for checking for understanding. This method is ideal for students who are benefiting from NIM, but still fail to attend to the meaning of the text. When students know that the intervention ends with questions, it might help students focus on the meaning of the text, which is the goal of reading.

> *When students know that the intervention ends with questions, it might help students focus on the meaning of the text, which is the goal of reading.*

The final strategy we discuss in this chapter is a hybrid of repeated readings and NIM that we call Read Two Impress (R2I) (Young, Mohr & Rasinski, 2015). This method focuses on word recognition, rate, and expression. The method begins with assisted reading and subsequently requires students to practice on their own. This method is ideal for students who struggle with rate, word recognition, and expression. In addition, it helps students who have trouble applying their knowledge of fluency instruction. It provides support so that immediately following the assisted reading, which models adult-like reading, the students have an opportunity to practice what they have learned.

Though we have made some recommendations, there is no one method that works for every child, especially those who require Tier 3 instruction. We encourage you to experiment with these methods, assessing frequently to determine the power and effectiveness of the intervention. When in doubt, ask the students which one they would like to try; it is possible that the added buy-in might be the key to achieving the gains necessary to help students read on grade level and beyond.

Repeated Readings

This method of intervention requires students to practice reading texts several times in an effort to increase accuracy and reading rate. The teacher and/or student select a text, and the student reads it four times while the teacher notes errors and records the student's reading rate. Extensive research supports this method as an effective means for developing students' reading fluency (Samuels, 1979; Therrien, 2004).

Background

Samuels (1979) first described the method of repeated readings in a study that he conducted with students with reading disabilities. He had students read a passage seven times, and with each reading, their reading rate increased and word recognition errors decreased. More importantly, he found that the practice transferred to new texts, and students demon-strated increased rate and accuracy on independent passages. Reading a text seven times may be somewhat monotonous, and fortunately, further research (Therrien, 2004) suggests that four readings are often sufficient. Still, reading a text four times may bore students as well, so we encourage you to consider materials and monitoring as two crucial details that make the method a bit more engaging.

Materials and Procedures

First, text selection is important. To prevent students from becoming bored by texts, make sure you choose high-quality, engaging texts. Good litera-ture works very well here. Also, due to the nature of the activity, we recom-mend using poetry or short stories. Poetry lends itself to fluency instruction as it is rich with prosodic elements, and it is meant to be read several times. You can use classic children's poetry (which you can find on the "Classical Poetry for Children" page on the Story It website), more modern children's poetry, or our (Chase's actually) favorite—humorous poetry (which you can find at the Giggle Poetry website).

Secondly, we know that many children (and adults) are motivated by success, so we recommend that you monitor each reading graphically. Time each reading while marking any word recognition errors, and then record them. We have used line graphs (Figure 4) and bar graphs (Figure 5) in the past and found the visual representation of their progress to be motivating for students. Feel free to adapt them or create new ones to meet the needs of your students (or to match your classroom decor).

Lower Elementary Grade Example

You are a second-grade teacher and are concerned about one of your students, Kacy. She reads slowly and pauses frequently to decode words. She is reading about one year below grade level (middle of first grade) and according to the running record, she is reading at about 30 words per minute with 95 percent accuracy in word recognition. Her expression is proficient (3) according to the Multidimensional Fluency Scale (see page 16), and she is adequate in comprehension. Kacy is beginning to notice that she is not reading like her peers and continues to struggle with grade-level texts, so her reading confidence is low.

The method of repeated readings might be a good fit based on this student's profile because of her low reading rate and borderline accuracy percentage. Slow reading can limit a student's ability to comprehend text (LaBerge & Samuels, 1974), so perhaps in this case, it will be important to focus on rate. Speed does matter, but it is not a race (Rasinski, 2000). We do not want you to create a NASCAR reader—one who flies through his or her reading at unimaginable rates for the sake of speed alone. We do, however, want readers to move along at an appropriate pace that is conducive for comprehension. In addition, the accuracy percentage is close to the instructional range, as anything below 95 percent makes it difficult for students to read independently (Clay, 2004). The practice element in this method should help you increase the student's accuracy.

Now that you have analyzed the students' data and determined that repeated readings might benefit the student, it is time to plan the intervention. Here are a few items you need to consider:

- Timeline
- Text selection
- Monitoring system
- Assessment

FIGURE 4 Line Graph

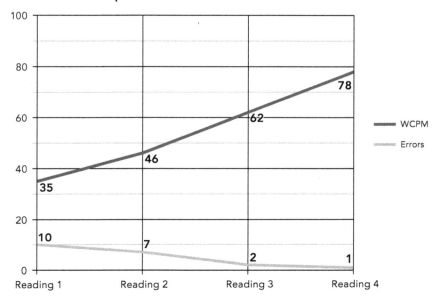

FIGURE 5 Bar Graph

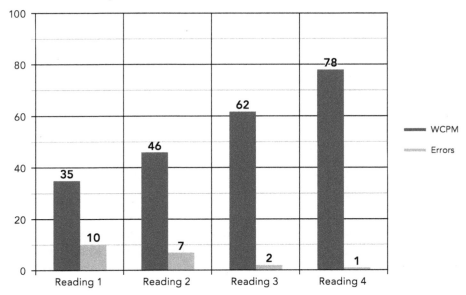

We recommend that you allow at least three to four weeks before reassessing the student to check the effectiveness of the intervention. Ideally, you should meet with the student every day for about 15 to 20 minutes. We realize that is an ambitious goal, so try to meet with your student at least three times per week but increase the time to around 30 minutes. Younger students may not be able to handle 30 minutes of repeated reading, so you may want to schedule a break or decrease the time slightly.

Next, consider the texts for the intervention. You need to choose these based on the student's interests. In this case, Kacy loves humorous poetry, so you might begin with *My Noisy Brother* by Bruce Lansky. (It is an added bonus that Kacy has a little brother and can easily relate to the poem.) Make sure the poem is not too easy or too difficult by using a reading level estimation program. These are available online, or you can copy and paste text into Microsoft Word and get the reading level after running a spelling and grammar check. According to this quick (but not completely accurate) test, *The Land of Nod* by Robert Louis Stevenson has a Flesch-Kincaid Level of 1.6 (first grade, sixth month) and is likely close to Kacy's instructional reading level.

Kacy is motivated by success and really enjoys art, so she might prefer the bar graph. Explain to Kacy how to complete the graph and what it means. Then, print two copies of the text, one for each of you. Time her reading while marking any word recognition errors on your copy. Let's say Kacy reads the text for the first time in 140 seconds with five errors. There are 76 words in the poem, so in order to calculate her Words Correct Per Minute (WCPM), use the following formula: WCPM x 60/seconds. In this case ($71 \times 60 / 140$), Kacy read at a rate of 30.43 WCPM. Ask Kacy to complete her bar graph by coloring in 30 WCPM and five errors for the first reading. Repeat this process for the next three readings. Kacy will then have a graphic representation of her progress.

Each time Kacy meets with you, she reads a text four times and keeps track of her own progress with your help. At the end of the intervention timeline, use the same assessment to determine Kacy's growth. Remember, this intervention targets WCPM and accuracy, so you should see the most gains in those dimensions. However, we recommend you assess all the dimensions of reading, including the third component of reading fluency, prosody. If Kacy is making adequate progress, continue with the interventions. However, if she is still developing too slowly to close the gap between herself and the reading expectations of second graders, consider alternate interventions.

Adaptations

The repeated readings method is easily modified for all ability levels. Simply by changing the text difficulty, you can effectively deliver the intervention to any student who struggles with fluency. However, for higher grade levels, you might consider choosing longer texts to help build reading stamina. Other modifications might include increasing or decreasing the number of readings, based on the student's ability to meet the expectations. For example, if a student consistently reads at an appropriate pace and with 95 percent accuracy after three readings, there is no need to ask him or her to read the text again. Conversely, adding a couple extra readings might be necessary for students who require a bit more practice. If you are also concerned about reading comprehension, you can ask students to retell the story after the first and last reading. Students will likely be able to produce a more detailed retelling after repeated practice. If you use a retell rubric, you can even represent the growth graphically as we did with rate and accuracy.

Effectiveness

There is a plethora of research out there on the effectiveness of repeated readings (Mathes & Fuchs, 1993; Mercer, Campbell, Miller, Mercer & Lane, 2000; Vadasy & Sanders, 2008; Vaughn, Chard, Bryant, Coleman & Kouzekanani, 2000). We personally have used this method with many disfluent readers. In some cases, students make one year's growth in only 10 weeks (Mohr, Dixon, Young & 2012), and in other cases, there is much more growth. There is nothing better than choosing an intervention that works, and this one works with a lot of disfluent readers. Then again, there is something better—the day your student reads alongside his or her peers with excellent fluency and bolstering confidence.

Neurological Impress Method

The Neurological Impress Method (NIM) is a form of calibrated choral reading whereby a teacher and student sit side by side and prepare to read a text. The teacher and student engage in a form of choral reading with the teacher reading slightly ahead of the student, essentially having the student follow closely behind the teacher's reading. In the dominant ear of the student, the teacher reads aloud with good expression.

Background

Heckelman summarized NIM in 1966. Later, Heckelman (1969) found that the NIM method actually "etched" the teacher's words and expression into the student's brain. In other words, after engaging in NIM, the student read more like the teacher. Decades were paved with NIM's positive results (Arnold, 1972; Cook, Nolan & Zanotti, 1980; Eldredge, 1990; Eldredge & Butterfield, 1986; Eldredge & Quinn, 1988; Henk, 1981; Hollingsworth, 1970; Hollingsworth, 1978; Langford, Slade & Barnett, 1974; Topping, 1987b). Despite early support for NIM, the method is not often used today.

> *In other words, after engaging in NIM, the student read more like the teacher.*

Materials and Procedures

NIM research recommends that you select a text at the student's independent reading level. Although we have also seen great success when using more challenging text, we will first explain the method derived from early research, which recommends easy texts. Following are the basic instructions for NIM.

1. Select a text.
2. Sit side by side with the student.
3. Begin reading aloud together.
4. Increase your pace so that you read slightly ahead of the student and read aloud with good expression.
5. Continue steps 2–4 for approximately 20 minutes.

Lower Elementary Grade Example

David is a second grader who reads at a first-grade level. He reads accurately but very slowly and with little expression. You use NIM to develop his fluency. Select a text with an approximate first-grade level. Begin by explaining the method in kid-friendly terms. For example:

1. We will begin reading the book together out loud.
2. I will then read a little bit faster, so I will be a bit ahead of you.

3. Let me know if you need a break.

4. We will keep doing this for 20 minutes.

For younger students, we recommend that you use one book and point to the words as you read them aloud. This will help the student stay focused and on track. In some cases, you might ask the student to place his or her hand on yours as you move through the text. Because you are only reading slightly ahead (no more than one syllable), pointing to the words as you read shouldn't confuse the students because you are still reading the same word. Some students in the lower grades may not be able to engage in NIM for the entire 20 minutes, so either give breaks or decrease the time to 10 or 15 minutes per day. Also, remember, this is a powerful method, so after a few meetings, you may want to reassess your student and increase the text difficulty.

Upper Elementary Grade Example

Yvette is a fourth grader reading at a third-grade level. Similar to the lower grades example, she reads accurately but very slowly and with little expression. You believe NIM might help develop her fluency because of its modeling and assisted components.

Because Yvette is in the fourth grade, you might also worry about her reading stamina. This approach might help build her stamina so that she can read for longer periods of time. Even though older students are better equipped to stay focused, we only increased the time to 30 minutes. In our experience, third, fourth, and fifth graders were able to engage in NIM for longer periods of time. Essentially, give them as much as they can handle.

Select a text at Yvette's independent reading level. Get two copies of the same text, so you and the student can each have one. In addition, fourth and fifth graders may not appreciate sharing a book while you point to the words. Begin by explaining the procedures in kid-friendly language. For example:

1. We will begin reading the book together out loud.

2. I will then read a little bit faster, so I will be a bit ahead of you.

3. Let me know if you need a break.

4. We will keep doing this for 30 minutes.

Adaptations

The easiest way to modify NIM is to adjust the time. If students get tired, give them a break or reduce the number of minutes. If they seem to handle it well, you might try to increase the time spent on NIM. Another way to modify this strategy is to adjust the text difficulty. In our recent research (unpublished at this time), we found that many students, including first graders, can engage successfully in NIM using texts that are approximately one year above their independent reading level. As mentioned before, however, the teacher or tutor needs to monitor the student very carefully.

Effectiveness

NIM can increase students' accuracy in word recognition and builds more expressive readers (Eldredge, 1990; Eldredge & Butterfield, 1986; Eldredge & Quinn, 1988; Henk, 1981; Hollingsworth, 1970; Hollingsworth, 1978; Topping, 1987b). According to the first study, Heckelman (1969) provided struggling readers with 7.25 hours of NIM training and saw a mean increase of 1.9 years in students' reading levels. Subsequent research confirms that NIM is an effective method for increasing students' reading fluency (Hollingsworth, 1970; Hollingsworth, 1978; Langford, Slade & Barnett, 1974; Topping, 1987a).

Neurological Impress Method Plus

The Neurological Impress Method Plus (NIM+) follows the same steps as NIM but has an additional comprehension component. After engaging in NIM, students retell the story and answer comprehension questions.

Background

Despite NIM's positive effects on students' reading fluency and overall ability (Arnold, 1972; Cook, Nolan & Zanotti, 1980; Eldredge, 1990; Eldredge & Butterfield, 1986; Eldredge & Quinn, 1988; Henk, 1981; Hollingsworth, 1970; Hollingsworth, 1978; Langford, Slade & Barnett, 1974; Topping, 1987b), the method disappeared from the literature for decades. Flood, Lapp, and Fisher (2005) noted this and inferred that perhaps NIM had also disappeared from the classroom and reading clinics. Thus, the researchers revisited NIM but added a comprehension component, an addition they called NIM+.

Materials and Procedures

First, as with NIM, Flood, Lapp, and Fisher (2005) recommend that you choose a book at the student's level, but they also recommend that you steadily increase the text difficulty as the student becomes more comfortable with the procedure. You could potentially increase the level each week or every few days. Indeed, this steady increase may extend into the student's frustration range. If the student does, indeed, become frustrated, we recommend you drop a level. Again, it is a careful calibration that only you can adjust because it is entirely based on your observations of the student during NIM+.

> You could potentially increase the level each week or every few days. Indeed, this steady increase may extend into the student's frustration range. If the student does, indeed, become frustrated, we recommend you drop a level. Again, it is a careful calibration that only you can adjust because it is entirely based on your observations of the student during NIM+.

In addition, because of the comprehension component, you will need to develop reading comprehension questions before each session. If time is an issue, you can always search for ready-made questions online. We recommend that you prepare at least five questions that are a mix of literal and inferential questions. That is, some questions might only require students to recall information from the text, where more inferential questions require students to interpret or process information from the text. Here are the basic steps for NIM+:

1. Select a text.
2. Prepare at least five comprehension questions (mix of literal and inferential).
3. Sit side by side with the student.
4. Begin reading aloud together.

5. Increase your pace so that you read slightly ahead of the student, and read aloud with good expression.

6. Continue for 15 to 30 minutes.

7. Ask the student to retell the story.

8. Ask the reading comprehension questions.

Lower Elementary Grade Example

A second-grade teacher, Dr. Fleming, has a student named Connor who could really benefit from intense fluency instruction. He reads slowly and laboriously, and his oral reading is monotone and lacks expression. Dr. Fleming knows that NIM might help with Connor's reading difficulties, but she also knows that Connor is struggling with comprehension, which is the main goal of reading. Fortunately for Dr. Fleming, NIM+ enhances both fluency and comprehension. According to the research she has read, NIM+ tends to have an effect on reading fluency and comprehension after 3.3 hours of tutoring. Thus, she plans to meet with Connor for 20 minutes five times per week for three weeks.

Dr. Fleming selects one copy of an appropriate text and prepares six comprehension questions, three literal and three inferential. She sits down side by side with Connor and explains the procedure to him:

1. We will begin reading this book together out loud.

2. Then I will read a little bit faster, so I will be a bit ahead of you.

3. We will keep doing this for 15 minutes.

4. After we finish reading, you will tell me what happened in the story.

5. Finally, I will ask you six questions about what you read.

Thus, the entire procedure takes about 20 minutes. Fifteen are for NIM, and the final five focus on the "plus" in which Connor retells what he has read and answers some questions.

Upper Elementary Grade Example

Mr. Perez teaches fifth grade, and one of his students, Erica, demonstrates reading difficulties, specifically in reading comprehension and fluency. Mr. Perez chooses NIM+ as her intervention. He plans to meet with her three times per week for 30 minutes each time. He will reassess her progress in four weeks. Mr. Perez selects two copies of an appropriate text and prepares 10 comprehension questions, six literal and four inferential. He sits next to Erica and explains the NIM+ procedure. For older students, the procedure takes about 30 minutes.

1. We will begin reading this book together out loud.

2. Then I will read a little bit faster, so I will be a bit ahead of you.

3. We will keep doing this for 25 minutes.

4. After we finish reading, you will tell me what happened in the story.

5. Finally, I will ask you 10 questions about what you read.

Adaptations

Similar to NIM, the easiest and most common way to adapt this method is to change the duration. Students who can participate for longer, should. Those who find it difficult to maintain a good pace for extended amounts of time might need a reduction. The comprehension component is also flexible. You can increase or decrease the number of questions as well as the nature of the questions. For example, if a student needs additional practice inferring, then you can increase the number of inferential questions.

Effectiveness

We know that NIM can effectively increase reading fluency (Arnold, 1972; Cook, Nolan & Zanotti, 1980; Eldredge, 1990; Eldredge & Butterfield, 1986; Eldredge & Quinn, 1988; Henk, 1981; Hollingsworth, 1970; Hollingsworth, 1978; Langford, Slade & Barnett, 1974; Topping, 1987b). Specific research on NIM with an added comprehension component revealed that the method can also increase reading comprehension. In a study by Flood, Lapp, and Fisher (2005), 20 students in grades three through six received 3.3 hours of NIM+. After five weeks, the results indicated that students who received the NIM+ treatment outperformed the control group's oral reading rate, silent reading rate, and reading comprehension.

Read Two Impress

Read Two Impress (R2I) is a one-on-one strategy that aims to enhance reading expression, accuracy, and pace. R2I is a hybrid of NIM and repeated readings. The tutor (a capable adult) and student first engage in NIM, where the tutor and student read aloud while the tutor reads slightly ahead of the student. Afterward, the student rereads the text aloud independently. Research on R2I suggests that the method can rapidly increase reading fluency and students' overall reading proficiency (Young, Mohr & Rasinski, 2015; Young & Mohr, 2016; Young, Rasinski & Mohr, 2016).

Background

We first used R2I with a couple of third graders who struggled with reading (Mohr, Dixon & Young, 2012). The students were not making progress with other interventions, but they showed some progress with repeated readings. However, the students still read with limited expression, and we felt NIM (Heckelman, 1969) might be a good next step. In light of the progress made with repeated readings, we were hesitant to conduct repeated readings, so we decided to integrate both strategies. As a result, both students made remarkable growth (Young & Mohr, 2016).

Since then, we conducted a quasi-experimental study with 51 third-, fourth-, and fifth-grade students. Students who received the R2I treatment outperformed the control group on several measures, including reading expression, automaticity in word recognition (rate), and overall reading proficiency (Young, Mohr & Rasinski, 2015).

Materials and Procedures

In order to select the appropriate text, you must first assess the student's independent reading level. Then locate a text that is approximately one year above the instructional reading level. You might be thinking that the text may be too difficult, which is true, but we provide the student with a lot of support, thus making it possible for the student to achieve success on a much higher level. Of course, if the student finds the text difficult despite your support, you can always find a more suitable text. Conversely, if the student reads effortlessly, you may want to increase the level to maximize the impact of R2I. After text selection, meet with the student one-on-one and execute the following steps:

1. Obtain two copies of the same text.

2. Begin reading the text together out loud.

3. Increase your pace, so you are reading slightly ahead of the student.

4. Stop after reading a paragraph or page.

5. Ask the student to reread the text.

6. Move on to the next paragraph or page and repeat the strategy.

7. Use the intervention at least three times per week, and assess progress after four weeks.

Lower Elementary Grade Example

Riley is a third-grade student in your classroom who struggles with reading. He is currently reading at a level 2.0, which means he is reading at least one year below his grade level. To prepare for R2I, you need to find a text that is close to a 3.0. You can choose any type of text or any genre. For this example, we use *Stellaluna* by Janell Cannon. It is a level 3.0 picture book that might suit Riley's interests. We recommend that you look at the text and determine appropriate stopping points—the point where you cease NIM and ask the student to reread. Because this is a picture book, and there are not too many words on each page, we suggest that you chunk the text by page.

Sit next to Riley, make sure he has his copy of the book, and introduce it. Next, in kid-friendly language, describe what you are about to do. For example, you might say, "We are going to read this book in a very special way. We will begin reading at the same time and read out loud. But, soon after, I will begin to read a little bit faster than you. Your job is to 'chase' me, but if you catch up, I am going to read a little bit faster. We will stop at the end of each page, and you can read it back to me."

When Riley is ready, begin reading out loud together. When you determine his pace, begin reading slightly faster than him. Of course, his pace will vary, so it is important to listen to him and adjust your pace to ensure you are only reading slightly ahead of him. In addition to reading at a decent pace, you also want to read with great expression. You are essentially providing a model of good fluent oral reading so that Riley can internalize the expression and use it later in his rereading. It is a tricky process and it might feel strange for you and Riley, but you will get used to it. In our experience, it takes about two or three sessions before everyone is comfortable.

After completing the page, ask Riley to reread the page out loud. You will notice that he reads rather automatically and at a good pace, and you will likely hear your modeled expression in his voice. After he rereads, move to the next page, and repeat this for at least 20 minutes. If Riley's rereading is disfluent, you may have to chunk the text into smaller sections, so you might reduce it to half of the page before he rereads. If he still struggles, you may need to find a slightly easier book. The goal is to provide enough assistance on a challenging text to support Riley's fluent reading.

Upper Elementary Grade Example

A fifth grader in your class, Stephanie, is nearly two years behind, according to her reading level of 3.4. You assessed her, and she is a prime candidate for R2I. Because of her high reading level, you might consider using a novel for the intervention text. You note that she loves to have fun in class, and other students find her humor amusing (even if you find it distracting). So you suggest *Class Clown* by Johanna Hurwitz. Because this is a novel, there are a lot of words on one page, so we suggest that you chunk the text by paragraphs rather than pages.

Similar to the lower grades example, introduce the book and explain the procedure to Stephanie. You might say, "We are going to read *Class Clown* out loud together. We will start together, but then I will read slightly faster than you. Your goal is to 'chase' me. We will stop after each paragraph, and you can read it back to me."

Begin reading out loud together. Listen to her pace, and begin reading slightly faster. As mentioned in the lower grades example, her pace will fluctuate, so make the adjustments to stay slightly ahead of her. Remember to read with appropriate expression, so she can "hear" the unwritten rules of expressive reading. Repeat for at least 20 minutes; however, with older students, you could increase this to 30 minutes.

Adaptations

R2I is a versatile intervention. You can use any type of text in any language and at any reading level. Depending on the student, you can modify this strategy to fit their needs. You can deliver this intervention anywhere between three and five days per week. Remember, we use this method to rapidly increase students' reading abilities and fluency, so it is important to increase the text level as often as possible. As soon as the student is competently rereading the text aloud, move on to a higher level. In addition, if you would like to add a comprehension component, feel free to engage the student in discussion after each rereading or at the end of each session.

Effectiveness

We have used this method with many struggling readers, many of which made remarkable progress. The original case studies describe two students who made two years of growth in eight weeks. In our next study, we used this strategy with 27 students and 88 percent made more than the expected gains after four weeks of R2I (Young, Mohr & Rasinski, 2015). In a recent program review, several students made two years of reading growth in six weeks. It may not always work with every student, but we have found that students who struggle with fluency can benefit greatly from R2I.

Conclusion

Tier 3 is essentially an educational emergency. The interventions you personally deliver could change the life of a child forever. We sincerely hope that one of the interventions described helps facilitate the transition from struggling reader to thriving reader. Assess your students often to determine the effectiveness of the intervention. In our experience, if you don't see some growth in four weeks, you may want to consider a different intervention. If the student is indeed making growth, continue the intervention until the child meets his or her reading goals. Nothing makes an RTI meeting greater than recommending a child be dropped from Tier 3 to Tier 2. It means that you have changed the educational trajectory of your student and ensured his or her future success in school and in life.

CHAPTER 5:

INTEGRATING TECHNOLOGY INTO READING FLUENCY INSTRUCTION

The final part of this book describes technologically enhanced fluency methods. We offer several different ways to tweak research-based strategies and increase the engagement factor with a bit of technology. These activities range from simply recording students so they can assess themselves to students making their own movies. Each activity is founded on strong fluency research and revamped to meet the needs of 21st century learners. The activities are quite versatile in that you can choose to implement most of them in whole group, small group, or one-on-one settings. Thus, you could potentially use the methods for Tier 1 and 2 interventions. Some of these activities require students to use the Internet for research. Discuss Internet safety with students prior to working on these activities. You may also choose to work with students, especially younger ones.

Recording Software for Fluency Development

Researchers (Hudson, Lane & Pullen, 2005) have found that recording software is helpful in developing students' reading fluency. In this method, students read aloud while being recorded. The recording is then played back so the student can hear his or her oral reading. We follow this with a discussion that allows the student to reflect on what he or she heard. Subsequently, the student rehearses the passage once, then records his or her reading, and listens again.

Background

Recording software can be used to develop students' reading fluency. Sometimes students are unaware of their disfluent reading. Fortunately, using recording software can be an objective means of providing unbiased feedback to a student. The method of repeated readings is certainly effective (Samuels, 1979), but the only one listening to the student is the teacher. There is a movement in literacy research that calls for self-assessments in hopes of students' involvement empowering them to excel (William, 2011). New technology makes it easier than ever to involve students in their evaluation of oral reading.

> *Sometimes students are unaware of their disfluent reading. Fortunately, using recording software can be an objective means of providing unbiased feedback to a student.*

Materials and Procedures

Select an instructional-level text appropriate for the student who is in need of fluency development. Make sure to have some sort of recording software or device. Begin recording and signal the student to start reading. At the conclusion of the reading, play the recording back to the student. After the student listens to his or her reading, ask him or her to reflect. At this point, we do not provide feedback to our student; instead, we allow the student to draw his or her own conclusions and conduct a critique. We are simply there to listen. After listening to the student's reflection, give him or her an opportunity to rehearse the reading. When the student is ready, record the reading again. Play the final version back to the student. Again, ask the student what he or she thought. Hopefully, you will hear him or her talk about the differences, but in some cases the student may note a need for further improvement. That is OK, too. In fact, that indicates the student is willing to continue the intervention. Now you have buy-in.

All Grades Example

Recently, a graduate student in a reading diagnosis course was unsure of an effective corrective action. Her third-grade student demonstrated adequate comprehension, did well in other subjects, and had a great attitude toward school, but her oral reading was riddled with errors and lacked expression, and she, in our opinion, read too fast. During a meeting with the teacher, we asked her whether the student was aware of her disfluent reading. We suggested the teacher record the student's playing and play it for her, which she did. The student was, to say the least, appalled. She immediately reread the text, paying closer attention to accuracy and her expression. After several rehearsals, she read expressively, accurately, and at a decent pace. Because of this initial success, we decided to continue the procedure. Three days per week, the student was recorded and required to listen to her reading. She then practiced once, and rerecorded her reading. After seven weeks of this intervention, her fluency for both accuracy and expression increased to the acceptable range, her reading rate went down (she was reading far too fast before), and her overall reading ability increased by 1.5 years. She demonstrated amazing growth with a simple recording strategy. Of course, it is not always that simple, but because of the simplicity of this method, it might not be a bad first choice for intervention.

Adaptations

In a more intense version of this method, students can record their first reading of a text and then listen while marking errors and making notes about expression on their copy of the text. Then they record their reading again. After recording their reading, they listen to the reading, mark errors, and make any notes for the next recorded reading. The student can continue this until the oral reading is error free and read with the desired expression.

Effectiveness

The student referenced above increased from a Developmental Reading Assessment (DRA) 24 to 38 in seven weeks. Her comprehension, as measured by a retelling, ascended from the adequate to advanced category. Her confidence soared, and, most important, she kept loving school. This by far is the most compelling evidence that practice-based methods are a viable means to increase reading fluency (Kuhn & Stahl, 2003; National Institute of Child Health and Human Development, 2000). In addition, including students in the assessment process and encouraging them to self-assess can be motivating (William, 2011).

Avatars for Speeches

Students use their voices to create avatars that read speeches. In this strategy, students rehearse a speech and read it aloud into avatar software (online or smartphone application). The final product is an avatar reading a speech.

Background

On the premise that practice makes better, students who rehearse famous (or infamous) speeches are afforded the opportunity to spend time developing accurate and expressive oral reading (Young & Rasinski, 2009). Like many of the performance-based strategies, rehearsing for a purpose increases the authenticity of the activity (Young & Nageldinger, 2014), thereby promoting engagement (Guthrie & Wigfield, 2000). In addition, the added technological component will also likely increase engagement (Jones & Brown, 2011). Thus, using avatars with speeches is a technological integration that builds fluent readers in a way that is meaningful and engaging.

Materials and Procedures

Students select speeches they want to rehearse and perform. You or your students can find speeches in print and/or digitally online. Refer to Chapter 2, pages 29–34, for the full explanation and procedure of using speeches in the classroom as an approach to fluency instruction. Next, you need to locate an avatar application or online site.

1. Access a website where students can build avatars and record their voices (i.e., Voki).

2. Students create an avatar that looks similar to the person who originally delivered the speech.

3. Students press "record" and read their speeches aloud into a microphone.

4. Students press "stop" when complete.

5. Students listen to the recording and assess for quality.

6. Students save the completed avatar speech under the teacher's profile.

7. Share via e-mail, website, or with the class.

Lower Elementary Grade Example

Mr. Austin is a third-grade teacher who is on a team that participates in a living museum activity. Students in third grade research a famous historical figure and select one of the figure's speeches or monologues to rehearse. After substantial rehearsal, each student dresses as his or her famous person to help create a living museum in the library. Parents and other students in the school visit the living museum and wander around listening to famous speeches orated by the students who are dressed for the part. This year, however, Mr. Austin wanted to add an intermediary step that allowed the students to first assess themselves delivering the speech before the big day.

The day before the living museum, Mr. Austin's class visited the computer lab. He showed students how to access the avatar website and gave a brief mini-lesson on how to manipulate the avatars to look like their chosen famous person. He allowed his students ample time to make the necessary adjustments to their avatars and readied them for the recording process. He showed them how to record and asked them to begin. After all of the students finished, he asked them to listen (we recommend headphones) to their speeches and assess whether their expressiveness captured the original speaker's intended meaning or purpose. If not, he asked them to rerecord their speeches. Essentially, the students self-assessed their reading fluency and made necessary adjustments through multiple rehearsals, which was the main goal of the activity. Now students were ready to perform in the living museum. The students did not save the avatars or post them; it was simply an engaging technology integration implemented to help students refine their speech performances.

> *The students did not save the avatars or post them; it was simply an engaging technology integration implemented to help students refine their speech performances.*

Upper Elementary Grade Example

After rehearsing speeches in the five-day format (described on pages 32–33), Ms. Kristen's fifth graders gathered around for a mini-lesson on creating avatars. She used the Voki website, which is free for teachers and allows students to save their avatars under their teacher's profile. She showed the students how to create the avatars in the image of their chosen speakers and how to record or rerecord, if necessary. Students were encouraged to rerecord if they felt they could do better. For homework over the weekend, Ms. Kristen required students to access the website, sign in under the class account, create their avatars, and save their final speeches. Students who preferred to create their speaking avatars at school could meet in the library on Monday morning for the first few minutes of class to complete their assignment (mostly for students who lacked technology at home). Because the speeches were saved, she played one speech per day at the beginning of class. Ms. Kristen also gave the login information to parents and relatives so that they could watch their student's speech.

Adaptations

There exists a variety of avatar software ideal for this strategy—the trick is finding the program that is right for you and your students. Some sites have full-body avatars, and you can choose backgrounds and other features, while other sites simply have the talking head. You can choose based on how detailed you want the avatars to be. For students who find this difficult, we recommend helping them with the technology aspect. However, if it is the text that is difficult, we suggest using students' selected speech as the material for any one of our Tier 2 or Tier 3 methods described in the book. Using these interventions might give them the practice, assistance, and modeling necessary to read the text expressively and accurately. In addition, it is possible that the actual speech is available in audio or video format online and could be used as a model for the student.

Effectiveness

National standards require that technology be integrated, so why not integrate it with strategies that are proven to work? The added technology will boost the engagement factor and perhaps increase the quality of the overall result. Though no conventional studies have been conducted on this specific method, its underlying premise is well researched. Students who engage in repeated readings (Samuels, 1979) and practice for a performance (Young & Rasinski, 2009) participate in an authentic classroom activity that promotes motivation (Guthrie & Wigfield, 2000). Added technology meets the needs (and wants) of 21st century learners (International Reading Association, 2009).

Explain Everything for Book Trailers

For this strategy, students use screencasting software to produce book trailers. They are like movie trailers but are created to provide a preview of a book. Students read a text, write a script, and digitize it using screencasting tools, such as Explain Everything. The purpose of the activity is for students to demonstrate their understanding of texts by using their expressive reading to create a suspenseful preview of the text.

Background

Educators believe that creating book trailers can pull kids into reading (Bates, 2012). Furthermore, Dalton and Grisham (2013) call for increased digital responses to literature. Thus, we decided to heed both calls by asking students to respond to literature digitally by creating book trailers. In addition, the writing and rehearsing of scripts, along with the performance component, promotes oral reading fluency.

Materials and Procedures

Explain Everything is an application that allows users to create slideshows using graphics, drawings, or pictures. The user then narrates each slide. Students can easily convert their completed projects into movies that they can save on the device or share in a variety of different ways, such as via YouTube or e-mail. There are other applications similar to Explain Everything, including programs like PowerPoint, and we encourage you to use whichever application you prefer. In addition to a screencasting application, you will also need books and devices that have the desired application installed. Following are the general procedures.

1. Students read a text.

2. Students write a brief summary of the text and leave out the ending.

3. Students turn their summary into a script.

4. Students rehearse the script until they can read it accurately and with appropriate expression.

5. Students use a screencasting tool to create slides that match their summary.

6. Students narrate each slide.

7. Students save their production in a movie format.

8. Students share their production with the world (optional).

Lower and Upper Elementary Grade Example

Two students decided to work together to create a book trailer for *Maybelle in the Soup* by Katie Speck. After learning about book trailers, including their style, content, and purpose, the students began working on the iPad and discussing some guiding questions.

Should I use pictures from the Internet, my own drawings, or pictures that I take? The students decided to use drawings and pictures from the Internet. In the introduction, the students stated that Maybelle was a cockroach that lived under the refrigerator, and they decided to use multiple photographs for the illustration. They copied and pasted a cockroach and a refrigerator from the Internet and moved them around to fit the oral description.

Do my illustrations match my narrative? The students carefully drew and utilized pictures from the Internet to match exactly what they were narrating. For example, on one slide, the students quoted the Peabodys from the book when they talked about no messes or bugs. The students created a corresponding illustration in Explain Everything using a combination of photos from the Internet and drawing. They drew an "X" over photos of dust, a messy room, and bugs and wrote "No" above them.

Have I practiced my narration? The students read and reread their lines, much a like a rehearsal for a performance. They even decided that in some spots, they would read in unison and in others, take turns. After watching the final video with its good elocution that entertained audiences, it was clear the students practiced. In this case, the students shared the book trailer on the teacher's class YouTube channel. Students 1 and 2 created the following script for their book trailer:

Student 1: There are two main characters. Their names are Maybelle and Henry.

Student 2: There are two evil characters as well. Their names are Mr. and Mrs. Peabody.

Students 1 & 2: They always say no to dust, messes, and bugs.

Student 1: Maybelle wants to taste something that has not hit the floor.

Student 2: The next day, the Peabodys made mock turtle soup. Maybelle wanted to try it and almost got spotted.

Students 1 & 2: Will she survive or will she be caught? Read *Maybelle in the Soup* to find out. Don't forget to read *Maybelle in the Soup* by Katie Speck!

Adaptations

We provided a basic description of book trailers, but you could certainly do so much more. For example, instead of drawing or importing pictures on each slide, you could have students recreate scenes and pose as a tableau while another student takes the picture. Students can do this with each slide and then complete the narration. If students struggle with the strategy, it helps to complete the entire process as a class first, perhaps several times, before handing over the responsibility to the students. However, when students are able to complete the task independently, creating book trailers makes an engaging workstation or center activity.

Effectiveness

The task provides a digital experience that requires students to engage in multiple literacy processes. For example, students are essentially creating detailed summaries (National Institute of Child Health and Human Development, 2000) and leaving out the resolution of the story in order to create suspense. In order to render a quality production, students need a deep understanding of the text. Students also engage in an authentic writing experience, focusing on embedding voice into their writing (Culham, 2011; Dorfman & Cappelli, 2007). In addition, the need for expression in the narration requires students to use their voices to convey the appropriate meaning and tone of the story, which promotes students' oral reading fluency.

Webcasts for Content-area Literacy

For this strategy, students conduct research on a topic and write research reports. The students then convert the reports into a script. Students rehearse their scripts to prepare for filming. After the rehearsal, students film and produce a webcast to teach the world about their topic.

Background

New Information and Communication Technologies (ICTs), or new available technology that allows for global communication, have had a large impact on literacy instruction in the 21st century (International Reading Association, 2009; Leu & Kinzer, 2000; Leu, Kinzer, Coiro & Cammack, 2004). Researchers insist that integrating these new technologies into the curriculum is essential in engaging learners in the digital age (International Reading Association, 2009; Lankshear & Knobel, 2006; Zawilinski, 2009). This strategy engages young learners in literacy processes enhanced by technology while adding a performance component that requires fluent oral reading (Young & Nageldinger, 2014).

Materials and Procedures

You will need Internet access, moviemaking software, and a group of creative students. Free moviemaking software is typically already on your computer or device. For example, Mac products come equipped with iMovie, and Windows PC products usually have Movie Maker. What follows are the general steps to creating a webcast for content-area literacy. These steps will be explained in detail in the classroom example section.

1. Choose a topic.

2. Students research the topic via the Internet or books.

3. Students write a research report.

4. Students create scripts for a news report that will demonstrate their learning.

5. Students rehearse their lines.

6. Students film their webcast.

7. Students download the footage onto a computer or device and use moviemaking software to edit and produce their webcast.

8. Students upload their webcast to the Internet (optional).

Lower Elementary Grade Example

This example comes from a second-grade classroom that studied king penguins. First, we gave the students a graphic organizer to aid in their research (see Figure 6 on page 94). In the computer lab, students used search engines and other websites to complete the graphic organizer. They used this information to write their final reports.

FIGURE 6 Graphic Organizer

Physical Description (height, weight, color, etc.)	Habitat
Diet and Predators	Interesting Facts (at least 3)

We provided several mini-lessons on how to write topic sentences, follow with important details, and write conclusions to each paragraph. You can teach this step in whatever way works best for your students. Once the students went through the entire writing process, they wrote their final drafts. We will use one student's paper as an example for completing the strategy.

In order to prepare for the scripting process, you need to think creatively. In this second-grade example, we put students into five groups and assigned each group a different job for the newscast. See Figure 7 below for the configuration.

FIGURE 7 **Research and Correlations to Webcast**

King Penguin Research Section	News Team Department
Webcast Framework	Anchors
Diet	Investigative Reporters
Habitat	Weather
Interesting Facts	Penguin Expert Consultants
Physical Description	Sports

The first group was assigned as anchors, making them responsible for creating the framework for the webcast. They essentially had to write a script that would help provide the direction and flow of the news. Their script was not derived directly from the research; the anchors wrote their script from scratch. They began with an introduction:

Anchor 1: Welcome to the King Penguin News. Here are five investigative reporters with some breaking news.

As you can see, the anchors decided to begin the news segment with the investigative reporters who were responsible for creatively conveying the interesting facts as if they were involved in some serious investigative reporting. They created a script from the research that they had done (Figure 8). You may notice that not all of the facts are present in the examples provided; that is because the groups of students used each of the reports to synthesize the information for the script.

FIGURE 8 King Penguin Diet

Research Report	Student Script
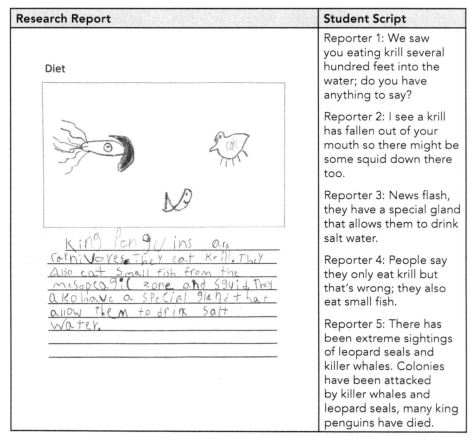Diet King Pengu ins are carnivores. They eat Krill. They Also eat Small fish from the mesopea gic zone and squid. They also have a special gland that allow them to drink Salt water.	Reporter 1: We saw you eating krill several hundred feet into the water; do you have anything to say? Reporter 2: I see a krill has fallen out of your mouth so there might be some squid down there too. Reporter 3: News flash, they have a special gland that allows them to drink salt water. Reporter 4: People say they only eat krill but that's wrong; they also eat small fish. Reporter 5: There has been extreme sightings of leopard seals and killer whales. Colonies have been attacked by killer whales and leopard seals, many king penguins have died.

The webcast then shifted back to the anchors, who introduced the next news segment.

Anchor 2: That was some interesting news, don't you think?

All Anchors: Uh-huh.

Anchor 3: Good thing we weren't there.

Anchor 1: How's the weather today, guys?

The anchors decided to go the weather next, where we learn about the king penguins' habitat. You can see how they used the research to create the script in Figure 9.

FIGURE 9 King Penguin Habitat

Research Report	Student Script
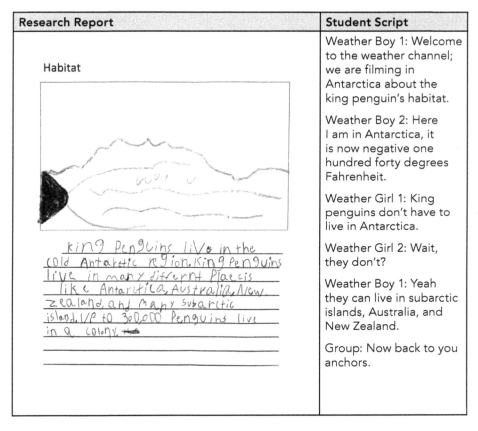 Habitat king Penguins live in the cold Antaretic region. King Penguins live in many difrernt Plaecis like Antaretica, Australia, New zealand, and many subarctic island. Up to 300,000 Penguins live in a colony.	Weather Boy 1: Welcome to the weather channel; we are filming in Antarctica about the king penguin's habitat. Weather Boy 2: Here I am in Antarctica, it is now negative one hundred forty degrees Fahrenheit. Weather Girl 1: King penguins don't have to live in Antarctica. Weather Girl 2: Wait, they don't? Weather Boy 1: Yeah they can live in subarctic islands, Australia, and New Zealand. Group: Now back to you anchors.

Yet another clever and quick change orchestrated by the anchors beginning with a reference to the freezing weather team.

Anchor 2: Don't forget to wear your heavy feathers.

Anchor 3: Here are some penguin experts and some interesting news.

A group of king penguin experts disseminated the information from the interesting facts section.

FIGURE 10 King Penguin Interesting Facts

Research Report	Student Script
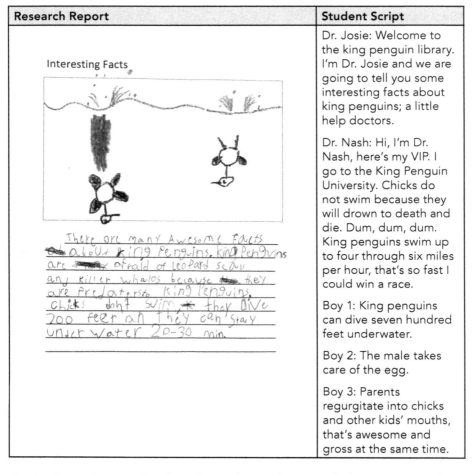	Dr. Josie: Welcome to the king penguin library. I'm Dr. Josie and we are going to tell you some interesting facts about king penguins; a little help doctors. Dr. Nash: Hi, I'm Dr. Nash, here's my VIP. I go to the King Penguin University. Chicks do not swim because they will drown to death and die. Dum, dum, dum. King penguins swim up to four through six miles per hour, that's so fast I could win a race. Boy 1: King penguins can dive seven hundred feet underwater. Boy 2: The male takes care of the egg. Boy 3: Parents regurgitate into chicks and other kids' mouths, that's awesome and gross at the same time.

Again, the script went back to the anchors, who provided a segue into the next segment, sports.

Anchor 1: That makes me want to buy a penguin.

Anchor 2: Hey let's check in with sports.

The sports team was charged with the difficult task of integrating the physical description into their segment. In our opinion, they did a wonderful and humorous job that resulted in a successful segment.

FIGURE 11 King Penguin Physical Description

Research Report	Student Script
The King Penguin: A Research Report by _____R i L e y_____ Physical Characteristics The K Penguin looks like the EMPeror Penguin. the ~~Emp~~ king Penguin is the 2nd largest Penguin because it can be 3 Feet tall and weigh 35 POUds, Adults ake grayish-black with orange on their beak and nect. Chicks are covered with Brown fur.	Sports Boy 1: Welcome to sports at five. Sports Boy 2: Keeping you up to date with all the latest sporting events. Sports Girl: Thanks for joining us. Sports Boy 1: First the King Penguin basketball team beat the rock hoppers. Sports Boy 2: The King Penguins were wearing their black and white jerseys while sporting some snazzy orange beaks. Sports Girl: It was quite the beating. Sports Boy 1: You can say that again. Sports Girl: It was quite the beating.

Sports Boy 1: Enough—The King Penguins basketball team was unable to beat the emperors.

Sports Boy 2: The emperors are the only larger species.

Sports Girl: Yeah the King penguins can't dunk.

Sports Boy 1: Why?

Sports Boy 2: Because they are only 3 feet tall and 35 pounds.

Sports Girl: It was quite the beating.

Sports Boy 1: Okay, back to you anchors.

Finally, the anchors conclude the webcast.

> *All Anchors:* Thanks for checking in on the King Penguin News.

> *Boy:* You stay classy, Maverick Elementary.

After the script was created, the students rehearsed their lines to ensure their expression would entertain audiences. To prepare for filming, the students rewrote their scripts on large poster paper that we kept behind the camera. These posters served as their cue cards. We filmed each segment and uploaded the footage onto computers in the classroom. Each group took turns editing their segments. Because each segment took multiple takes, the groups discussed the best takes and included them in the final production. Our class had special permission from parents to upload the video to the Internet, so they could share their learning with the world.

Adaptations

If your students struggle with the process, we suggest that you complete the task as a whole group. For example, you can conduct the research with your students and complete a research report through shared writing. As a class, you can create the script and separate students into different news teams. Then, as in our example, film the webcast as a class.

Effectiveness

We engaged students in research and writing, followed by the complex task of creating a script from text (Young & Rasinski, 2011). Then students rehearsed their lines, a method proven to enhance reading fluency (Young & Rasinski, 2009). Finally, the students used technology to make their learning come alive via a webcast, a method similar to student-produced movies (Young & Rasinski, 2013) but with a nonfiction focus.

Podcasting for Reader's Theater

For this strategy, students rehearse reader's theater and audio record their performances. After recording, the students can upload the file to the Internet. Therefore, the audience extends beyond the classroom and is accessible worldwide.

Background

Reader's theater is a popular activity proven to increase students' reading fluency as well as their engagement (Young & Rasinski, 2009). With the wide availability and versatility of technology, Vasinda and McLeod (2011) suggest an engaging way to integrate technology with reader's theater. The students rehearse daily, similar to other reader's theater designs, but on the final day, the students audio record their oral performances and upload them to their class blog. The researchers added this engaging integration to expand the audience for students and also to serve as the authentic purpose for participating in repeated readings, a strong approach to building reading fluency (Samuels, 1979).

Materials and Procedures

Reader's theater scripts can be found all over the Internet and are also available for purchase, both in print and digital formats. You need to select several scripts for each week, so multiple groups can rehearse different scripts. For the technology integration, you need some form of recording software. It is easiest to use freeware on computers to make the uploading process run smoothly. If you use separate recording devices, you will need a way to download them onto the computer, smartphone, or tablet you wish to later upload from. Having students speak directly into the microphone attached to the computer or other device cuts out that downloading step.

Use the format described in the reader's theater section found in Chapter 2, pages 34–40, of this book. Have the students rehearse daily. The structure is exactly the same until the final day. Instead of the students performing for a live audience, use the following procedures:

1. Each group of students gathers around the recording device.
2. Press "record."
3. Students begin the performance.
4. Press "stop."
5. Save the recording.
6. Listen to the recording to ensure quality.
7. Rerecord if necessary.
8. Upload the audio file to the class blog or other website (optional).

Lower Elementary Grade Example

Ms. Vasinda's second graders just completed their four days of rehearsal and are ready to record their performances. On Fridays, which is performance day, Ms. Vasinda has center time in the afternoon. She has students rotate through various centers, one of which is the recording center, where Ms. Vasinda is prepared to help the students record their performances and upload them to her class's private blog.

She first asks her students to engage in a final rehearsal and listens for quality. She might chime in on occasion to correct inaccurate pronunciations or to coach students' expression. Once Ms. Vasinda is satisfied, she positions the students around the microphone attached to her laptop. She opens the recording software, presses "record," and signals the students to begin. She presses "stop" after the performance and replays the recording for students. She encourages students to listen for quality and lets them know that it's OK if they want to record another take. If the students are satisfied, she helps them upload the file to the performance day blog post. Relatives around the globe can then tune in and listen to the masterpieces.

Upper Elementary Grade Example

After rehearsing throughout the week, Mr. Smith's fourth graders are ready to record their performances. Mr. Smith checked out five iPads from the library, one for each reader's theater group. In Mr. Smith's class, all of the groups work independently to record their performances. They use screencasting software, such as Explain Everything, Fotobabble, or PowerPoint. Although there is plenty of software out there from which to choose, Mr. Smith chooses a classic, PowerPoint.

The students only need to create one slide before the performance. As a group, the students decide on one photo that might represent the script they intend to perform. For example, if they were set to perform *Sleepover Safari* by Lucinda Cotter, they might add a picture of animals on the savanna, perhaps lions or giraffes. Then the students narrate the slide with their performance. After the initial recording, the groups replay their recordings and assess the quality of the sound and expressiveness of the reading. The groups save their final take and upload it to the class website, so parents, friends, and relatives around the world can download the file and listen to amazing students integrate technology with a timeless reading fluency activity.

Adaptations

The method is easily modified by controlling the text difficulty. In addition, you can choose to share students' recordings in any way you are comfortable. If you have a website and parent consent, feel free to post them for the world to view. However, if you are not comfortable, posting to a private blog is an easy way to safely share your students' work. Also, you could simply e-mail the files to parents, so they can control who can listen. If you are using screencasting software, you could also increase the number of slides required so that the performances resemble digital storytelling.

Effectiveness

Vasinda and McLeod (2011) implemented reader's theater podcasting for 10 weeks with 100 second- and third-grade students in a Title I school. Thirty-five of the participants were identified as struggling readers, and those students made an average of 1.13 years of growth in 10 weeks. Teachers and students found the activity both motivating and challenging.

Student-produced Movies as Authentic Fluency Development

This strategy has students producing motion pictures based on mentor texts. The students engage in a complex process of turning a book into a movie, a practice that engages students in multiple literacy steps, utilizes technology, and requires students to read aloud fluently.

Background

It is imperative that we engage students in motivational literacy experiences that utilize technology (International Reading Association, 2009). This strategy meets that requirement by creating an authentic and motivating literacy experience. When students create movies from mentor texts, they must have a clear understanding of the text and the author's voice in order to bring the book to life on the silver screen (Young & Rasinski, 2013).

> *When students create movies from mentor texts, they must have a clear understanding of the text and the author's voice in order to bring the book to life on the silver screen* (Young & Rasinski, 2013).

Materials and Procedures

You will need mentor texts, storyboards (Figure 12), a video-recording device, and a computer or handheld device with moviemaking software. On PCs, you will find Windows Movie Maker; Macs have iMovie. If you are using a handheld device, there are numerous applications you can download to edit your movies. It takes nine steps to complete the student-produced movie. What follows are the general steps, which we explain in the classroom example.

1. Students choose a group based on a preferred mentor text.

2. Students create a script treatment, which is essentially a summary of the text, a list of necessary materials, and student roles (i.e., director, camera person, cast, etc.).

3. The teacher meets with students to make sure they chose a suitable text, assigned roles, and have a good understanding of the text.

4. Students complete storyboards for each scene.

5. Using the mentor text, students create a script for each scene.

6. Students rehearse their scripts until fluent and expressive.

7. The teacher conferences with students prior to filming to ensure that all materials can be obtained and to set up the filming date and schedule.

8. Students film their movie.

9. Students use editing software to produce their movie.

FIGURE 12 Storyboard

Movie Title: _____   Scene: _____

Camera View:

Additional Information:

Characters:	Materials:	Filming Location:

Lower Elementary Grade Example

Mr. Parsons begins the student-produced movie process with his second-graders by asking students to form groups based on a genre of their choice. It's loud, it's chaotic, but it's necessary. The students roam the room inquiring about possible movie projects until they settle into a group that fits their interest and cinematic vision. Because it was Mr. Parsons first time implementing the strategy in the classroom, the grouping process took longer than usual—nearly 20 minutes. However, he wanted to ensure that students had the opportunity to make the right decisions.

Next, the groups discuss the mentor text they would like to use as a basis for their movie. Again, this takes some time. It is important that each group is happy with the text selection because they will spend a great deal of time working on the project. When each group is settled, Mr. Parsons announces that this would be the last chance to change groups. He does this because he knows that some students may have been happy with the genre but perhaps unhappy with the text selection. Mr. Parsons gives choices to get buy-in from students, an important factor necessary for completing the complex process of this strategy.

Mr. Parsons is satisfied. The groups are settled, and he asks that each write a script treatment. *Script treatment*, in this context, is another term for summary. This aspect makes Mr. Parsons particularly happy because he has struggled for years to find an engaging way to ask students to write summaries for an authentic purpose. However, student-produced movies changed that, and his students tend to view summaries in the context of movie production more positively.

Along with creating the summary, students assign their roles. Although the role assignments are mostly up to the students, Mr. Parsons makes sure that everyone has a part, and most importantly, that everyone is capable of being successful in their roles. That's right—Mr. Parsons knows his students and whether they will work well together in their assigned roles. For example, a student who always has to have it his or her way may not be the best choice for director. Thus, the teacher can "help" make decisions if necessary.

Students also list the materials needed for the movie. Mr. Parsons makes sure the materials are obtainable and school appropriate. Often he will suggest alternatives for groups who believe they require objects, such as toy helicopters. Mr. Parsons meets with the production groups and makes any adjustments necessary as well as provides suggestions that may help the group realize their cinematic visions. Once Mr. Parsons is satisfied, the kids get a "green light" or "go picture" and begin the next phase.

Students read and reread the text or text selection in order to complete the storyboards (Figure 12 on page 105). They discuss the required number of scenes, the camera angles for each scene, and the required materials and characters. To help students understand the required number of scenes, Mr. Parsons explains that any time they have to stop filming (i.e., press the "pause" button), one scene is complete. So students create a new story-board for each foreseen pause in filming. Students draw a picture of what each scene will look like and write down any additional information below the drawing. Not only will this give students a framework for production, but it will provide the director with the necessary information to guide the process.

After completing the storyboards, the students write a script for each scene. This is a complex process that requires students in the group to have a deep understanding of the text (Young & Rasinski, 2011). Students adhere to the storyline, preserve the author's purpose, and embed voice into the script. They turn narration into dialogue and eliminate erroneous descriptive text that will be apparent in the video. Mr. Parsons realizes that this is a difficult process, so he models writing the script until the students are ready to tackle it on their own.

Now that students have a script, Mr. Parsons encourages them to rehearse their lines. Much like reader's theater, students focus on correct word identification first and then shift their focus to expressive reading. Of course, Mr. Parsons wants this to sound more like a movie than a play, so he emphasizes regular speech rather than overly dramatic oral reading. Though Mr. Parsons does some voice coaching, he encourages the students in the group to coach each other as well. Thus, students strive for natural speech.

Once the students have assumed their desired voices, the groups meet with Mr. Parsons one more time to schedule filming. Along with the group, Mr. Parsons selects a day for filming and makes sure that all of the students bring the necessary materials. He explains that scenes will be filmed in between academic events. For example, students might film two scenes in between writer's workshop and independent reading, perhaps a few more before lunch, and a couple after recess. This will help break up the day, and because Mr. Parsons works with young students, he brings his entire class to each filming location. Breaking up the filming helps keep the other students from being bored—in fact, Mr. Parsons believes these breaks are actually quite good for the class. Plus, production teams get to watch how other teams engage in the filming process.

Adaptations

For younger students or students who find the process difficult, the teacher can serve as the director. This will help manage the group and ensure a quality product. There are many complex tasks in this strategy, so it is important to provide assistance whenever necessary. Remember, this is not a task that can only be "graded" if done independently; it is a group effort and requires a knowledgeable teacher willing to provide instruction and the scaffolding necessary to guide students to success. Thus, you might want to meet with groups who find the process difficult during each phase.

Effectiveness

Students who engage in the movie-production process find it to be a fun and engaging activity. They look forward to the project and are motivated to do a good job. This is great news for teachers because the process requires students to engage in several complex tasks. From beginning to end, students reflect on their reading preferences, produce summaries, create sequences, and engage in complex writing while transforming texts into scripts. In addition, through rehearsal, students read fluently and with appropriate expression. The entire process is an authentic and engaging activity that promotes reading fluency as well as other literacy processes, including media literacy. As an added bonus, students and their families can watch and re-watch their cinematic masterpieces until the end of time (Young & Rasinski, 2013).

Conclusion

We hope this chapter inspired you to enhance your classroom fluency instruction with technology. Certainly, it can be a lot of work, but we can attest that time and effort is well worth it. With technology, we can motivate students to engage in extremely complex tasks that can increase reading fluency and overall reading achievement. We have implemented all of the activities in elementary classrooms, and we have seen the success and engagement firsthand. Now, it is your turn. Enjoy.

Concluding Thoughts

According to Valencia and Buly (2004), 80 percent of students who experience reading difficulty struggle with at least one of the constructs of reading fluency—accuracy, automaticity, and/or prosody. Thus, we continue to research methods that effectively develop your students' reading fluency so that they can focus on the main goal of reading: comprehension. Fortunately for all of us, methods that target reading fluency can be engaging for students and fun to implement in the classroom. From read-alouds to student-produced movies, the goal of this book is to provide research-based strategies to increase your students' reading fluency. We know that fluent readers are more likely to comprehend what they read (LaBerge & Samuels, 1974; Rasinski & Young, 2014). We hope this book acts as a foundation for your fluency instruction so that your instruction can be a foundation for your students' reading proficiency.

RECOMMENDED FLUENCY RESOURCES

Allard, H. & Marshall, J. (1977). *Miss Nelson Is Missing!* Boston: Houghton Mifflin.

Barrett, J. & Barrett, R. (1982). *Cloudy with a Chance of Meatballs.* New York: Aladdin Books.

Bradby, M. & Soentpiet, C. K. (1995). *More than Anything Else.* New York: Orchard Books.

Child, L. (2005). *Clarice Bean Spells Trouble.* Cambridge, MA: Candlewick Press.

Cleary, B. & Zelinsky, P. O. (1983). *Dear Mr. Henshaw.* New York: W. Morrow.

Cleary, B. (1968). *Ramona the Pest.* New York: Dell Publishing.

Cronin, D. & Lewin, B. (2000). *Click, Clack, Moo: Cows that Type.* New York: Simon & Schuster Books for Young Readers.

Cronin, D. & Bliss, H. (2003). *Diary of a Worm.* New York: Joanna Cotler Books.

Curtis, C. P. (1997). *The Watsons Go to Birmingham.* London: Orion Children's Books.

Fleischman, P. & Beddows, E. (1985). *I Am Phoenix: Poems for Two Voices.* New York: Harper & Row.

Fleischman, P. & Beddows, E. (1988). *Joyful Noise: Poems for Two Voices.* New York: Harper & Row.

Fleischman, P. & Giacobbe, B. (2000). *Big Talk: Poems for Four Voices.* Cambridge, MA: Candlewick Press.

Fritz, J. & DePaola, T. (1987). *Shh! We're Writing the Constitution.* New York: Scholastic.

Gantos, J. (1998). *Joey Pigza Swallowed the Key*. New York: Farrar, Straus and Giroux.

Greene, R. G. & Smith, J. A. (2002). *Eek! Creak! Snicker, Sneak*. New York: Atheneum Books for Young Readers.

Griffin, J. B. & Tomes, M. (1977). *Phoebe the Spy*. New York: Scholastic Book Services.

Guarino, D. & Kellogg, S. (1989). *Is Your Mama a Llama?* New York: Scholastic.

Hollander, J. & Comport, S. W. (2004). *Poetry for Young People: American Poetry*. New York: Sterling Pub.

Katz, A. & Catrow, D. (2001). *Take Me Out of the Bathtub and Other Silly Dilly Songs*. New York: Margaret K. McElderry Books.

Katz, A. & Catrow, D. (2003). *I'm Still Here in the Bathtub: Brand New Silly Dilly Songs*. New York: Margaret K. McElderry Books.

Katz, A. & Catrow, D. (2005). *Where Did They Hide My Presents?: Silly Dilly Christmas Songs*. New York: Margaret K. McElderry Books.

Katz, A. & Catrow, D. (2006). *Are You Quite Polite?: Silly Dilly Manners Songs*. New York: Margaret K. McElderry Books.

Kimmel, E. A. & Docampo, V. (2009). *The Three Little Tamales*. New York: Marshall Cavendish Children.

Kinney, J. (2007). *Diary of a Wimpy Kid*. New York: Amulet Books.

Lansky, B. & Carpenter, S. (2004). *Miles of Smiles: A Collection of Laugh-Out-Loud Poems*. Minnetonka, MN: Meadowbrook Press.

Le Guin, U. K. & Schindler, S. D. (1988). *Catwings*. New York: Orchard Books.

Long, M. & Shannon, D. (2003). *How I Became a Pirate*. San Diego: Harcourt.

Lord, B. & Simont, M. (1984). *In the Year of the Boar and Jackie Robinson*. New York: HarperCollins.

MacLachlan, P. (1985). *Sarah, Plain and Tall*. New York: HarperCollins.

Marshall, J. (1987). *Red Riding Hood*. New York: Dial Books for Young Readers.

Mitchell, M. K. & Johnson, L. (1996). *Granddaddy's Gift*. Mahwah, NJ: BridgeWater Books.

Osborne, M. P. & McCurdy, M. (1991). *American Tall Tales*. New York: Knopf.

Prelutsky, J. & Stevenson, J. (1984). *The New Kid on the Block: Poems*. New York: Greenwillow Books.

Prelutsky, J. (2000). *It's Raining Pigs & Noodles*. New York: HarperCollins.

Prelutsky, J. & Cushman, D. (2006). *What a Day It Was at School!* New York: Greenwillow Books.

Rappaport, D. & Collier, B. (2001). *Martin's Big Words: The Life of Dr. Martin Luther King, Jr*. New York: Hyperion Books for Children.

Schachner, J. B. (2003). *Skippyjon Jones*. New York: Dutton Children's Books.

Schwartz, A. & Gammell, S. (1981). *Scary Stories to Tell in the Dark*. New York: Lippincott.

Scieszka, J. & Smith, L. (1992). *The Stinky Cheese Man and Other Fairly Stupid Tales*. New York: Viking.

Scieszka, J. & Smith, L. (1996). *The True Story of the 3 Little Pigs!* New York: Puffin Books.

Silverstein, S. (1981). *A Light in the Attic*. New York: Harper & Row.

Spinelli, J. (1996). *Crash*. New York: Random House.

Swados, E. & Cepeda, J. (2002). *Hey You! C'mere!: A Poetry Slam*. New York: Arthur A. Levine Books.

Viorst, J. (1987). *Alexander and the Terrible, Horrible, No Good, Very Bad Day*. New York: Simon & Schuster.

White, E. B. (1952). *Charlotte's Web*. New York: Harper & Brothers.

Willems, M. (2003). *Don't Let the Pigeon Drive the Bus!* New York: Hyperion Press.

Willems, M. (2003). *Knuffle Bunny: A Cautionary Tale.* New York: Hyperion.

Willems, M. (2006). *Don't Let the Pigeon Stay Up Late!* New York: Hyperion Books for Children.

Willems, M. (2008). *The Pigeon Wants a Puppy!* New York: Hyperion Books for Children.

Williams, V. B. (1982). *A Chair for My Mother.* New York: Greenwillow Books.

Yep, L. (2000). *Cockroach Cooties.* New York: Hyperion Books for Children.

Yolen, J. & Schoenherr, J. (1987). *Owl Moon.* New York: Philomel Books.

ADDITIONAL RECOMMENDED AUTHORS AND POETS

Brod Bagert

Paul Fleischman

David L. Harrison

Sara Holbrook

Alan Katz

Bruce Lansky

Kenn Nesbitt

Robert Pottle

Jack Prelutsky

Michael Salinger

Shel Silverstein

CHILDREN'S LITERATURE CITED

Cannon, J. (1993). *Stellaluna*. New York: Harcourt Brace.

Cotter, L. (2013). *Sleepover Safari*. Engage Literacy. North Mankato, MN: Capstone.

Cotter, L. (2013). *Wild Savanna Zoos*. Engage Literacy. North Mankato, MN: Capstone.

Hurwitz, J. (1987). *Class Clown*. Engage Literacy. New York: Scholastic.

Murphy, S. (2013). *The Team*. North Mankato, MN: Capstone.

Lansky, B. (1994). *My Noisy Brother*. In Lansky, B. (Ed.) *A Bad Case of the Giggles*. Minnetonka, MN: Meadowbrook Press.

Longfellow, H. W. (2001). *Paul Revere's Ride*. New York: Handprint Books.

Speck, K. (2007). *Maybelle in the Soup*. New York: Henry Holt and Co.

Stevenson, R. L. (1913). *The Land of Nod*. In Stevenson, R. L. (Ed.) *A child's garden of verses*. England, UK: Simon & Schuster Children's.

REFERENCES

Arnold, R. D. (1972). A comparison of the neurological impress method: The language experience approach, and classroom teaching for children with reading disabilities. Final Report. Lafayette, IN: Purdue Research Foundation. (ERIC Document Reproduction No. ED 073428).

Bates, N. (2012). Weaving a virtual story—creating book trailers 101. *Knowledge Quest, 40*(3), 72–76.

Chomsky, C. (1976). After decoding: What? *Language Arts, 53,* 288–296.

Clay, M. (2004). *Running records for classroom teachers.* Portsmouth, NH: Heinemann.

Cook, J. E., Nolan, G. & Zanotti, R. J. (1980). Training auditory perceptions problems: The NIM helps. *Academic Therapy, 15,* 473–481.

Culham, R. (2011). Reading with a writer's eye. In T. Rasinski (ed.), *Rebuilding the Foundation, Effective Reading Instruction for the 21st Century* (pp. 245–270). Bloomington, IN: Solutiontree.

Cunningham, P. M., Hall, D. P. & Sigmon, C. M. (2000). *The teacher's guide to the four blocks: A multimethod, multilevel framework for grades 1–3.* Greensboro, NC: Carson-Dellosa.

Daane, M. C., National Assessment of Educational Progress & National Center for Education Statistics (2005). *Fourth-grade students reading aloud.* Washington, DC: National Center for Education Statistics, U.S. Dept. of Education, Institute of Education Sciences.

Dalton, B. & Grisham, D. L. (2013). Love that book: Multimodal response to literature. *The Reading Teacher, 67*(3), 220–225.

Dorfman, L. R. & Cappelli, R. (2007) *Mentor texts: Teaching writing through children's literature, K–6.* Portland, ME: Stenhouse.

Eldredge, J. L. (1990). Increasing reading performance of poor readers in the third grade by using a group assisted strategy. *Journal of Educational Research, 84,* 69–77.

Eldredge, J. L. & Butterfield, D. D. (1986). Alternatives to traditional reading instruction. *The Reading Teacher, 40,* 32–37.

Eldredge, J. L. & Quinn, W. (1988). Increasing reading performance of low-achieving second graders by using dyad reading groups. *Journal of Educational Research, 82,* 40–46.

Fawson, P. C. & Reutzel, R. D. (2000). But I only have a basal: Implementing guided reading in the early grades. *The Reading Teacher, 54,* 84–98.

Flood, J. D., Lapp, D. & Fisher, D. (2005). Neurological Impress Method PLUS. *Reading Psychology, 26*(2), 147–160.

Ford, M. P. & Opitz, M. F. (2008). A national survey of guided reading practices: What we can learn from primary teachers. *Literacy Research & Instruction, 47*(4), 309.

Fountas, I. C. & Pinnell, G. S. (1996). *Guided reading: Good first teaching for all children.* Portsmouth, NH: Heinemann.

Fuchs, L. S., Fuchs, D. & Hosp, M. K. (2001). Oral reading fluency as an indicator of reading competence: A theoretical, empirical, and historical analysis. *Scientific Studies of Reading, 5*(3), 239–256.

Goldenberg, C. N. (1992). Instructional conversations: Promoting comprehension through discussion. *The Reading Teacher, 46,* 316–326.

Griffith, L. W. & Rasinski, T. V. (2004). A focus on fluency: How one teacher incorporated fluency with her reading curriculum. *The Reading Teacher, 58*(2), 126–137.

Gupta, A. (2006). Karaoke: A tool for promoting reading. *The Reading Matrix, 6*(2), 80–89.

Guthrie, J. T. & Wigfield, A. (2000). Engagement and motivation in reading. In M. Kamil, R. Barr, P. Mosenthal & D. Pearson. *Handbook of reading research III.* (pp. 403–425). New York: Longman.

Hasbrouck, J. & Tindal, G. A. (2006). Oral reading fluency norms: A valuable assessment tool for teaching teachers. *The Reading Teacher, 59,* 636–644.

Heckelman, R. G. (1966). Using the neurological impress remedial reading method. *Academic Therapy, 1,* 235–239.

Heckelman, R. G. (1969). A neurological-impress method of remedial reading instruction. *Academic Therapy Quarterly, 4,* 277–282.

Henk, W. A. (1981). Neurological impress and reading: How? And Why? Pittsburgh, PA: The Thirteenth Annual Three Rivers Reading Conference Proceedings. (ERIC Document Reproduction No. ED 220815).

Hollingsworth, P. M. (1970). An experiment with the impress method of teaching reading. *The Reading Teacher, 24,* 112–114.

Hollingsworth, P. M. (1978). An experimental approach to the impress method of teaching reading. *The Reading Teacher, 31,* 624–626.

Homan, S. P., Klesius, J. P. & Hite, C. (1993). Effects of repeated readings and nonrepetitive strategies on students' fluency and comprehension. *Journal of Educational Research, 87,* 94–99.

Hudson, R., Lane, H. & Pullen, P. (2005). Reading fluency assessment and instruction: What, why, and how? *The Reading Teacher, 58*(8), 702–714.

International Reading Association (2009). *New literacies and 21st century technologies: A position statement of the International Reading Association.* Newark, DE: Author. Retrieved March 21, 2015 from http://www.literacyworldwide.org/docs/default-source/where-we-stand/new-literacies-21st-century-position-statement.pdf?sfvrsn=6.

Iwasaki, B., Rasinski, T., Yildirim, K. & Zimmerman, B. S. (2013). Let's bring back the magic of song for teaching reading. *The Reading Teacher, 67*(2), 137–141.

Jones, T. & Brown, C. (2011). Reading engagement: A comparison between e-books and traditional print books in an elementary classroom. *International Journal of Instruction, 4*(2), 5–22.

Keehn, S., Harmon, J. & Shoho, A. (2008). A study of readers theater in eighth grade: Issues of fluency, comprehension, and vocabulary. *Reading & Writing Quarterly, 24*(4), 335–362.

Kuhn, M. R. & Stahl, S. A. (2003). Fluency: A review of developmental and remedial practices. *Journal of Educational Psychology, 95*(1), 3–21.

LaBerge, D. & Samuels, J. (1974). Towards a theory of automatic information processing in reading. *Cognitive Psychology, 6,* 293–323.

Langford, K., Slade, K. & Barnett, A. (1974). An examination of impress techniques in remedial reading. *Academic Therapy, 9,* 309–319.

Lankshear, C. and Knobel, M. (2006). *New Literacies: Everyday Practices and Classroom Learning* (second edition). Maidenhead and New York: Open University Press.

Leu, D. J. & Kinzer, C. K. (2000). The convergence of literacy instruction with networked technologies for information, communication, and education. *Reading Research Quarterly, 35*(1), 108–127.

Leu, D. J., Kinzer, C. K., Coiro, J., Castek, J. & Cammack, D. W. (2004). Toward a theory of new literacies emerging from the Internet and other informational and communication technologies. In R. B. Ruddell & N. Unrau (Eds.), *Theoretical models and processes of reading* (5th ed., pp. 1570–1613). Newark, DE. International Reading Association.

Martinez, M., Roser, N. L. & Strecker, S. (1998). "I never thought I could be a star": A readers theatre ticket to fluency. *The Reading Teacher, 52*(4), 326–334.

Mathes, P. G. & Fuchs, E. S. (1993). Peer-mediated reading instruction in special education resource rooms. *Learning Disability Research and Practice, 8*(4), 233–243.

McCauly, J. K. & McCauly, D. S. (1992). Using choral reading to promote language learning for ESL students. *Reading Teacher, 45,* 526–533.

Mercer, C. D., Campbell, K. U., Miller, M. D., Mercer, K. D. & Lane, H. B. (2000). Effects of a reading fluency intervention for middle schoolers with specific learning disabilities. *Learning Disability Research and Practice, 15*(4), 179–189.

Miller, J. & Schwanenflugel, P. J. (2006). Prosody of syntactically complex sentences in the oral reading of young children. *Journal of Educational Psychology, 98*(4), 839–853.

Miller, J. & Schwanenflugel, P. J. (2008). A longitudinal study of the development of reading prosody as a dimension of oral reading fluency in early elementary school children. *Reading Research Quarterly, 43*(4), 336–354.

Mohr, K. A. J., Dixon, K. & Young, C. J. (2012). Effective and efficient: Maximizing literacy assessment and instruction. In Ortlieb, E. T. & Cheek, Jr., E. H. (Eds.). *Literacy Research, Practice, and Evaluation: Vol. 1. Using informative assessments for effective literacy practices.* Bingley, UK: Emerald Group.

National Center on Response to Intervention (2010). *Essential Components of RTI—A Closer Look at Response to Intervention.* Washington, DC: Office of Special Education Programs, National Center on Response to Intervention, U.S. Department of Education.

National Institute of Child Health and Human Development (2000). *Report of the national reading panel. teaching children to read: An evidence-based assessment of the scientific research literature on reading and its implications for reading instruction* (NIH publication no. 00-4769). Washington, DC: U.S. Government Printing Office.

Opitz, M. F. & Rasinski, T. V. (2008). *Good-bye round robin.* Portsmouth, NH: Heinemann.

Padak, N. & Rasinski, T. (2005). *Fast Start for Early Readers: A Research-Based, Send-Home Literacy Program.* New York: Scholastic.

Padak, N. & Rasinski, T. (2008). *Fast Start: Getting Ready to Read.* New York: Scholastic.

Pearson, P. D. & Gallagher, M. C. (1983). The instruction of reading comprehension. *Contemporary Educational Psychology, 8,* 317–344.

Pinnell, G. S. & Fountas, I. C. (2007). *The continuum of literacy learning, K–8: Behaviors and understandings to notice, teach, and support.* Portsmouth, NH: Heinemann.

Rasinski, T. (2000). Speed does matter in reading. *The Reading Teacher, 54*(2), 146–151.

Rasinski, T. (2004). *Assessing reading fluency.* Pacific Institute for Research and Evaluation.

Rasinski, T. V. (2010). *The fluent reader: Oral and silent reading strategies for building word recognition, fluency, and comprehension* (2nd ed.). New York: Scholastic.

Rasinski, T. (2012). Why reading fluency should be hot. *The Reading Teacher, 65,* 516–522.

Rasinski, T., Blachowicz, C. L. Z. & Lems, K. (Eds.). (2012). *Fluency instruction: Research-based best practices* (2nd ed.). New York: The Guilford Press.

Rasinski, T. & Padak, N. (2004). *Effective reading strategies: Teaching children who find reading difficult.* Upper Saddle River, NJ: Merrill/Prentice Hall.

Rasinski, T., Padak, N., Linek, W. & Sturtevant, E. (1994). Effects of fluency development on urban second-grade readers. *The Journal of Educational Research, 87*(3), 158–165.

Rasinski, T., Rikli, A. & Johnston, S. (2009). Reading fluency: More than automaticity? More than a concern for the primary grades? *Literacy Research and Instruction, 48*(4), 350–361.

Rasinski, T. & Stevenson, B. (2005). The Effects of Fast Start Reading, A Fluency Based Home Involvement Reading Program, On the Reading Achievement of Beginning Readers. *Reading Psychology: An International Quarterly, 26,* 109–125.

Rasinski, T. & Zimmerman, B. (2011). Fluency: The misunderstood goal of the school reading curriculum. *School Library Journal,* Retrieved September 22, 2015, from http://www.slj.com/2011/05/standards/fluency-the-misunderstood-goal-of-the-school-reading-curriculum/.

Rinehart, S. (1999). Don't think for a minute that I'm getting up there: Opportunities for readers' theater in a tutorial for children with reading problems. *Journal of Reading Psychology, 20,* 71–89.

Samuels, S. J. (1979). The method of repeated readings. *The Reading Teacher, 41,* 756–760.

Samuels, S. J. (2002). "Reading fluency: Its development and assessment." In *What research has to say about reading instruction,* 3rd ed., A. E. Farstrup and S. J. Samuels (Eds.). Newark, DE: International Reading Association.

Schreiber, P. A. (1980). On the acquisition of reading fluency. *Journal of Reading Behavior, 7,* 177–186.

Therrien, W. J. (2004). Fluency and comprehension gains as a result of repeated reading: A meta-analysis. *Remedial and Special Education. 25*(4), 252–261.

Topping, K. (1987a). Paired reading: A powerful technique for parent use. *The Reading Teacher, 40,* 604–614.

Topping, K. (1987b). Peer tutored paired reading: Outcome data from ten projects. *Educational Psychology, 7,* 133–145.

Topping, K. (1989). Peer tutoring and paired reading. Combining two powerful techniques. *The Reading Teacher, 42,* 488–494.

Topping, K. (1995). *Paired reading, spelling, and writing*. New York: Cassell.

Tyler, B. & Chard, D. (2000). Using readers theatre to foster fluency in struggling readers: A twist on the repeated reading strategy. *Reading and writing quarterly. 16(2)*, 163.

Vacca, J., Vacca, R. & Gove, M. (2000). *Reading and learning to read* (4th ed.). New York: Longman.

Vadasy, P. F. & Sanders, E. A. (2008). Repeated reading intervention: Outcomes and interactions with readers' skills and classroom instruction. *Journal of Educational Psychology, 100*, 272–290.

Valencia, S. W. & Buly, M. R. (2004). Behind test scores: What struggling readers really need. *The Reading Teacher, 57*, 520–531.

Vasinda, S. & McLeod, J. (2011). Extending reader's theater: A powerful and purposeful match with podcasting. *The Reading Teacher, 64(7)*, 486–497.

Vaughn, S., Chard, D. J., Bryant, D. P., Coleman, M. & Kouzekanani, K. (2000). Fluency and comprehension interventions for third-grade students. *Remedial and Special Education, 21(6)*, 325–335.

Wilfong, L. G. (2008). Building fluency, word-recognition ability, and confidence in struggling readers: The poetry academy. *The Reading Teacher, 62(1)*, 4–13.

William, D. (2011). *Embedded formative assessment*. Bloomington, IN: Solution Tree.

Young, C. J. (2013). Repeated readings through readers theater. In Rasinski, T. & Padak, N. (Eds.). *From fluency to comprehension: Powerful instruction through authentic reading*. New York: Guilford Press.

Young, C. & Mohr, K. A. J. (2016). Successful literacy interventions: An RTI case-study analysis. In S. Garrett (Ed.). *CEDER Yearbook*. Texas A&M University-Corpus Christi: Center for Educational Development, Evaluation, and Research.

Young, C., Mohr, K. A. J. & Rasinski, T. (2015). Reading together: A successful reading fluency intervention. *Literacy Research and Instruction, 54(1)*, 67–81.

Young, C. & Nageldinger, J. (2014). Considering the context and texts for fluency: performance, reader's theater, and poetry. International Electronic Journal of Elementary Education, 7(1), 47–56.

Young C. & Rasinski, T. (2009). Implementing readers theatre as an approach to classroom fluency instruction. The Reading Teacher, 63(1), 4–13.

Young, C. & Rasinski, T. (2011). Enhancing authors' voice through scripting. Reading Teacher, 65(1), 24–28.

Young, C. & Rasinski, T. (2013). Student produced movies as a medium for literacy development. Reading Teacher, 66(8), 670–675.

Young, C., Rasinski, T. & Mohr, K. A. J., (2016). Read Two Impress: An intervention for disfluent readers. Reading Teacher.

Young, C., Valadez, C. & Gandara, C. (2016). Using performance methods to enhance students' reading fluency. Journal of Educational Research.

Zawilinski, L. (2009). HOT blogging: A framework for blogging to promote higher order thinking. The Reading Teacher, 62(6), 650–661.

Zimmerman, B., Rasinski, T. & Melewski, M. (2013). When kids can't read, what a focus on fluency can do. In E. Ortlieb and E. Cheek (eds.). Advanced literacy practices: From the clinic to the classroom (pp. 137–160). Bingley, UK: Emerald Group Publishing.

Zutell, J. & Rasinski, T. (1991). Training teachers to attend to their students' oral reading fluency. Theory into Practice, 30(3), 211–217.

NOTES

NOTES

Tiered Fluency Instruction: Supporting Diverse Learners in Grades 2–5

NOTES

Maupin House
capstone

At Maupin House by Capstone Professional, we continue to look for professional development resources that support grades K–8 classroom teachers in areas, such as these:

Literacy	Language Arts
Content-Area Literacy	Research-Based Practices
Assessment	Inquiry
Technology	Differentiation
Standards-Based Instruction	School Safety
Classroom Management	School Community

If you have an idea for a professional development resource, visit our Become an Author website at:

http://www.capstonepub.com/classroom/professional-development/become-an-author/

There are two ways to submit questions and proposals.

1. You may send them electronically to: proposals@capstonepd.com

2. You may send them via postal mail. Please be sure to include a self-addressed stamped envelope for us to return materials.

Acquisitions Editor
Capstone Professional
1 N. LaSalle Street, Suite 1800
Chicago, IL 60602